Joint Application Design

The Group Session Approach to System Design

Judy H. August

YOURDON PRESS
Prentice Hall Building
Englewood Cliffs, New Jersey 07632

Library of Congress Cataloging-in-Publication Data

August, Judy H. (Judy Hirschmann) (date)
    Joint application design :   the group session approach to system
design / Judy H. August
      p.   cm.   —   (Yourdon Press computing series)
Includes bibliographical references and index.
ISBN 0–13–508235–8 : $26.25
1. System design—Methodology. I. Title. II. Series.
QA76.9.588A84   1991   90-12895
004.2′1—dc20   CIP

Editorial/production supervision
  and interior design: Kathryn Gollin Marshak
Cover design: Lundgren Graphics Ltd.
Manufacturing buyers: Kelly Behr and Susan Brunke

 Published by Prentice Hall
A division of Simon & Schuster

Printed in the United States of America
10 9   8   7   6   5   4   3   2   1

ISBN   0-13-508235-8

Prentice-Hall International (UK) Limited, *London*
Prentice-Hall of Australia Pty. Limited, *Sydney*
Prentice-Hall Canada Inc., *Toronto*
Prentice-Hall Hispanoamericana, S.A., *Mexico*
Prentice-Hall of India Private Limited, *New Delhi*
Prentice-Hall of Japan, Inc., *Tokyo*
Simon & Schuster Asia Pte. Ltd., *Singapore*
Editora Prentice-Hall do Brasil, Ltda, *Rio de Janeiro*

To Jackie and Stacey

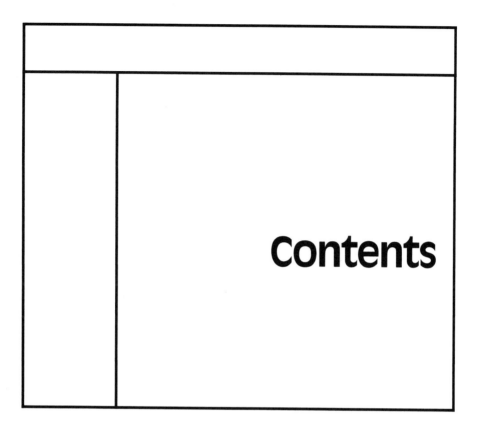

Contents

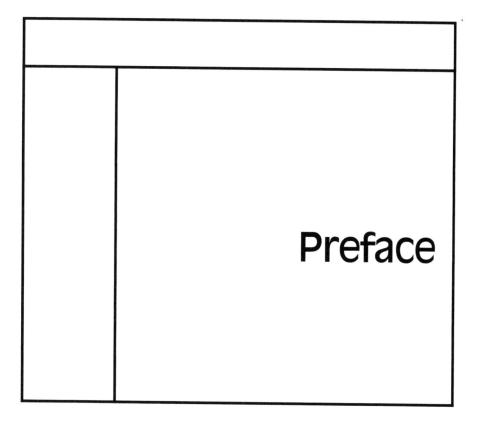

Preface

Joint Application Design (JAD) is a methodology that accelerates the design of computer applications. Guided by a session leader, users and information systems professionals design systems together in structured group sessions. JAD harnesses the creativity and teamwork of group dynamics to define the users' view of the system—from the system objectives and scope through screen and report design. JAD results in more usable systems, completed faster.

JAD was developed by IBM in 1977 and has been proven successful on hundreds of software projects across industry, hardware, and application boundaries. Currently, JAD is not only an IBM-sponsored methodology and a GUIDE (IBM user group) project, but is also backed by many consulting firms and software engineering authorities such as James Martin. It effectively dovetails with most other software development methodologies and computer-aided software engineering (CASE) tools. Organizations large and small have made JAD a way of life, incorporating it into their overall software development standards.

Because of JAD's significant achievements and success, interest in JAD spans across a broad spectrum of people. Some are directly involved in JAD projects, such as session leaders, users, information systems professionals, and management. Others are evaluating whether to attempt their first JAD. Still others are students or professionals seeking to expand their software development skills and enhance their marketability.

To accommodate these varying levels of interest in JAD, this book is organized into three modular sections:

SECTION I: JAD OVERVIEW

The first four chapters of this book provide the reader with a solid JAD foundation. Chapter 1 places JAD within the context of traditional methodologies in order to explain why JAD is unique. Whereas most development methodologies differ in the standards of diagrams and text they employ, readers will learn that JAD distinguishes itself by its entire philosophy and facilitated group design approach. Chapters 2 and 3 provide an overview of the structure, objectives, and outputs of JAD. Finally, Chapter 4 discusses the JAD participants, explaining their role in the process, as well as the qualities and experience they should possess.

SECTION II: HOW TO PERFORM A JAD

Chapters 5 through 10 provide a phase-by-phase description of each of the JAD tasks and outputs. These chapters serve as a comprehensive reference, providing details about the techniques and standards of the methodology. Case study examples and real-world experiences bring JAD to life. Practitioners can also benefit from productivity aids, such as checklists, agendas, documentation forms, and estimating worksheets.

SECTION III: PRACTICAL CONSIDERATIONS

The last two chapters provide essential information about JAD in practice. Chapter 11 focuses on session leader facilitation skills. It answers such questions as, How do you start a discussion? What do you do once it has begun? How do you recognize a "people issue," and how do you solve the problem? What session leader style is most effective? Chapter 12 addresses the activities, issues, and options involved in implementing JAD in an organization. It answers the question, If you like what you now know about JAD, where do you go from here?

JAD's innovations surprise most people who learn about them; expecting to read about some newfangled, off-the-wall concepts, they realize that JAD is a sound, commonsensical approach. It brings the users and information systems professionals together, enabling them to share their concerns and build on each other's expertise. It provides them with the tools, structure, and techniques to design a system more effectively and productively. JAD promotes teamwork, producing synergistic solutions and a strong commitment to the system's successful implementation.

Judy Hirschmann August

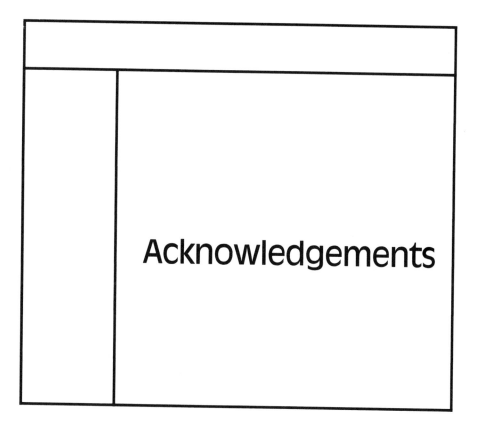

Acknowledgements

First, special thanks to the following family members and colleagues who reviewed the manuscript and helped me with this project: Harriet and Henry Hirschmann, Stanley August, Marti Wien, Pete Marcus, and George Henningsen.

I would also like to thank the individuals within IBM Professional Services for providing me with a wealth of JAD opportunities. The breadth of my JAD experience was largely made possible by people such as John Sisto, Mike Grich, Jim Martin, Lauren Evanco, Bill Levine, Phil Giordano, Tom Byrne, Mike Rider, and Jack Pascal.

Thanks to Carol Petok Bell, Robert Densen, and Carolyn Katz for their help on this project. And, finally, thanks to the Prentice Hall staff who helped to produce this book, including Paul Becker, Kathryn Marshak, and Noreen Regina.

Joint
Application
Design

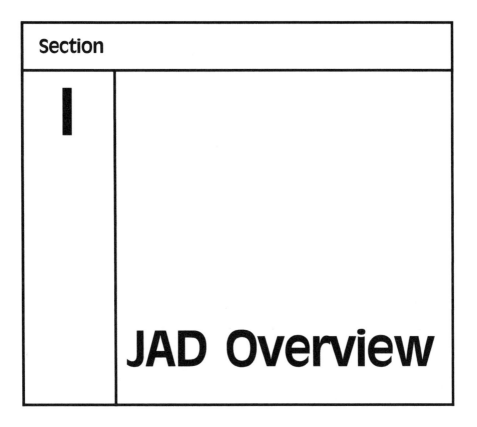

Section

I

JAD Overview

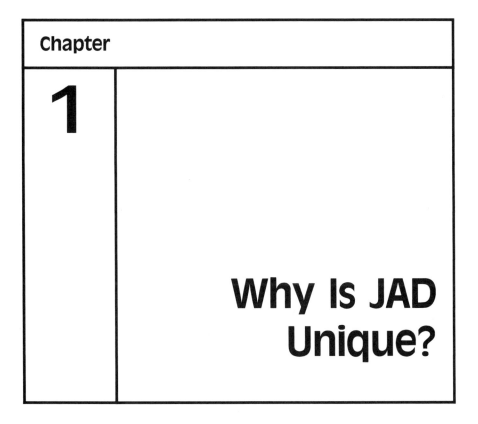

Chapter

1

Why Is JAD
Unique?

Software design methodologies abound. Each one comes to market claiming to be the new and improved product, with better diagrams, more appropriate text standards, and thorough, top-down analysis. So why has Joint Application Design (JAD) received so much attention and been so successful? What makes JAD unique?

Whereas most methodologies differ in the standards of diagrams and text they employ, JAD distinguishes itself by its entire philosophy and approach. JAD draws users and information systems professionals together to jointly design systems in facilitated group sessions. It takes an innovative, yet commonsensical, approach to the objectives, requirements, and external (user) design of software (see Fig. 1-1) and generates big payoffs:

- **Increased productivity.** Studies report 20 to 60 percent increases in productivity over traditional design methods [1]. These productivity gains are achieved on the basis of both calendar time and person-hours needed to complete the objectives, requirements, and external design phases.
- **Enhanced design quality.** Although many organizations initially try JAD for its productivity gains, users and information systems professionals who have

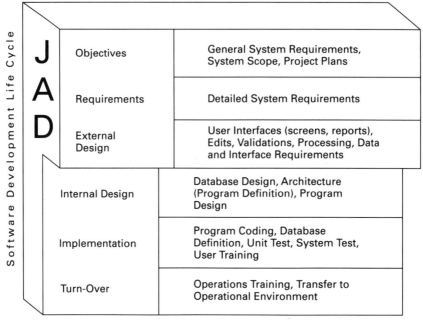

Figure 1-1 How JAD fits into the software development life cycle. JAD addresses the objectives, requirements, and external design phases of the life cycle.

had experience with JAD usually cite high-quality design as JAD's most significant benefit.

- **Teamwork.** JAD promotes cooperation, understanding, and teamwork among the various user groups and the information systems staff. Rather than fighting each other—in effect, subverting the development project—the players build on each other's expertise. Users and information systems professionals truly design the system together and become jointly committed to the successful development of the system.

- **Lower development and maintenance costs.** JAD's high-quality design provides a big paycheck during the technical phases of development and after the system is delivered. Study after study has shown that errors in defining the objectives, requirements, and external design are the most expensive to fix later on, typically incurring significant time and cost overruns.[1] JAD gets the

---

[1]Gary Rush states that "error removal constitutes up to 40% of the cost of a system. Between 45% and 65% of these errors are made in system design" [9, p. 11]. Likewise, James Martin cites one corporation which found that 64 percent of its bugs were in analysis and design even though the users had formally signed off on the documentation. He also notes that 95 percent of the cost of correcting bugs for a large bank project was for requirements and design errors [8]. Citing a Government Accounting Office study of nine software development projects, Charles Martin concludes that "less than 5 percent of the money put into the nine software developments resulted in software which could be used as delivered or with minor changes. . . . The report suggests that these systems were not properly described in the first place" [6].

design right the first time, thus eliminating most of the error-associated development and maintenance costs.

JAD accomplishes these results by harnessing group dynamics, making the design tangible through visual aids, providing an organized, rational process, and adhering to a "what you see is what you get" documentation approach (Fig. 1-2).

GROUP DYNAMICS

JAD unleashes the power and creativity of group dynamics to accomplish the objectives, requirements, and external (user) design efforts. Facilitated by an experienced JAD session leader, management, users, and information systems professionals work as a team in group sessions to analyze requirements, generate innovative ideas, and make decisions that shape the system design (Fig. 1-3).

JAD leaps beyond the traditional one-on-one and group interview format in which the information systems analysts collect data from the users but design the system themselves. It rejects the notion that the analysts can learn the many nuances of the users' jobs well enough to second-guess effectively, let alone productively, what users require in a system. JAD acknowledges the reality that even the most experienced users may not fully understand how their work affects other areas and levels of the organization; without the chance to share ideas and cross-educate themselves, users will typically generate requirements simply to automate the current operation rather than seizing the opportunity to improve the process.

JAD knocks down the obstacles to effective design. It places the users in the driver's seat. With strategic input from management and advice from information systems representatives, *users* create the design—from defining system objectives to designing the screen and report layouts. One idea builds on the next as the participants become committed to synergistic solutions to the organization's needs.

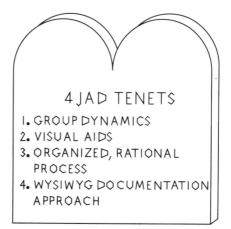

4 JAD TENETS
1. GROUP DYNAMICS
2. VISUAL AIDS
3. ORGANIZED, RATIONAL PROCESS
4. WYSIWYG DOCUMENTATION APPROACH

Figure 1-2 The four JAD tenets.

(a)   (b)

Figure 1-3   Group dynamics. The JAD participants share ideas and design the system as
a team. (a) Interview-based design methodologies. (b) JAD's group dynamics.

VISUAL AIDS

One of the barriers to effective user participation in the requirements and design
process has always been how to make requirements and design concepts more
tangible to the user (Fig. 1-4). All too often, users and information systems
professionals who seem to agree on the requirements and design concepts are at
odds when the system is actually delivered. Whether simply asking users to review
a design created by information systems professionals or, in the case of JAD,
allowing the users to shape their own systems, the challenge is to bring the concepts
into the realm of reality before spending the time and money to build the system.

JAD marshals numerous types of visual aids to make the design concepts
more tangible. In fact, the JAD visual aids temporarily transform the ordinary
conference room, ''wallpapering'' it from top to bottom with design references.
Special JAD magnetics, a prototype, flip charts, transparencies, and writing boards
serve to communicate and validate ideas better during the design process.

ORGANIZED, RATIONAL PROCESS

JAD adheres to the more traditional, nonparticipative design methodologies by
incorporating an organized, rational process. Although JAD effectively utilizes
brainstorming techniques to generate ideas, it has a more rigorous task structure and
is much more productive than pure brainstorming. JAD employs top-down analysis
and well-defined, phased tasks in order to accomplish the objectives, requirements,
and external design efforts (Fig. 1-5).

(a)

(b)

Figure 1-4 Visual aids. JAD effectively uses visual aids to make the design tangible. (a) Lack of visual aids can be misleading. (b) Visual aids help to communicate clearly.

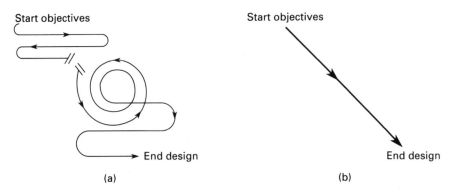

Figure 1-5 Organized, rational process. (a) Less structured efforts are plagued by problems such as backtracking, design gaps, and getting lost in the details. (b) JAD's process maps out a direct route to design completion.

Top-down analysis means analyzing the high-level, more general areas first before focusing on the details. Handling each level of detail sequentially helps to ensure thorough analysis for two major reasons: First, top-down analysis greatly reduces the chances of design gaps or holes. By defining the panorama of the system first, each successive level of detail may be related back to the overall picture and checked for completeness. For example, does the definition of system scope cover all of the requirements previously set forth? Does the list of screens, reports, system interfaces, and processing handle the entire system scope?

Second, by enforcing top-down analysis, each level of detail receives the appropriate amount of attention. The natural tendency in software design is to jump straight to the details, assuming that the high-level, broader topics are self-evident. What a faulty assumption! Reevaluating the more general topics affecting the system often produces the most significant, far-reaching innovations. It allows JAD participants to step away from the current environment and rethink the system target. What are the strategic and future considerations for the system? Are there any constraints or assumptions to be considered? By agreeing on the system target, the participants lay a foundation of common understanding upon which they can build the remainder of the design.

JAD helps to ensure top-down analysis by incorporating specific tasks and outputs that address each level of design detail in the appropriate sequence. Each task is well defined to make the entire process as organized and productive as possible. Although JAD contains a mechanism by which the session leader may tailor the output formats to meet an organization's existing standards, the modifications must fit in with JAD's structured, top-down process.

WYSIWYG DOCUMENTATION APPROACH

Each JAD produces an output document. The purpose of the document is to formally record the JAD results so that both users and information systems professionals may understand the decisions made: Users must be able to review carefully and approve the document contents as a quality assurance measure; information systems professionals must be able to readily access the information they need to perform the technical design, coding, and testing of the system. The JAD documents effectively communicate to both groups through a ''what you see (in session) is what you get'' (WYSIWYG) documentation approach.

Traditionally, the documents produced as phase outputs have done an excellent job in communicating the phase results to the technical team, but they have been alien and difficult to understand for the users. Some inroads have been made in this area through the use of more user-friendly diagram and text standards. However, much of the difficulty still remains largely because both the format of the document and the ideas expressed are unfamiliar to the users. In traditional methods, users must digest an enormous amount of new and conceptually challenging material. No wonder many a user has experienced heartburn upon seeing the voluminous documents delivered from information systems.

In contrast, the JAD WYSIWYG documentation approach ensures that both document content and format are completely familiar to users and information systems professionals alike. All of the ideas and decisions expressed in the document are generated in the facilitated JAD group sessions. All of the document formats (diagrams, fill-in-the-blank forms, and text) are presented and explained in session and are utilized throughout the session through visual aids.

The familiarity of the JAD documents reinforces the feeling of participant ownership and leads to a more effective review process. When the JAD session participants review a document, they recognize the material as their own. They do not have to struggle to comprehend the document but can concentrate on validating the accuracy and viability of the document's contents. Because the various user groups and the information systems group work together as a team to create the document, the review process is void of the usual politics, finger pointing, and infighting (Fig. 1-6). Instead, cooperation prevails. Everyone's goal is to produce the best document, one that they can be proud to call their own.

THE HISTORY OF JAD

How JAD Came to Be

Born out of frustration with trying to obtain user agreement on the requirements and design of distributed manufacturing systems (the old 8100 hardware), JAD was originally developed by IBM in 1977. It was seen as a way to develop consensus among a broad group of users. JAD caught on quickly, particularly in Canada where IBM performed JADs for its customers.

When IBM noticed the considerable success JAD achieved in Canada with its narrow, manufacturing focus, it assigned JAD to its U.S. professional services unit. As an employee of IBM's professional services unit at the time and one of its first session leaders, I was very much involved in the effort to merge the innovative JAD

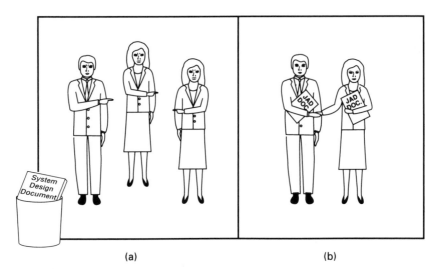

Figure 1-6   JAD's WYSIWYG documentation approach helps to avoid finger pointing
and promotes participant pride and commitment to the document.

techniques with IBM's proven software development methodology. In 1984, after
many trials and tribulations, IBM introduced a revamped JAD. The current version
of JAD described in this book applies across industry, application, and hardware
boundaries.

JAD is Evolutionary

Although JAD may be viewed as a major breakthrough for software design
methodologies, it is in fact a commonsensical, evolutionary development. Its broad
acceptance is a result of trends in both the software development discipline and in
the user community.

JAD builds on the structured analysis and software development life cycles
that emerged in the 1970s. It maintains their organized, phased approach but greatly
expands the user's role in the requirements and design process. The breakthrough of
the 1970s was to perform one-on-one interviews with users in order to understand
their requirements. However, the 1980s brought an awareness that the process
required even more user involvement. The information systems group became tired
of receiving the blame for completed systems that ostensibly reflected user-
approved designs but were in fact unsatisfactory to the users once delivered. As a
result, new, user-oriented documentation standards, prototyping, and group interviews were developed. JAD goes beyond these solutions by enabling users to define
their own objectives, requirements, and external design. Although information
systems professionals provide valuable advice during a JAD, the methodology
shifts the focus by placing the user at the controls.

JAD also applies the focus on productivity and quality to the creative process
of software design. JAD improves the way ideas are generated and decisions are

made in much the same way that computer-aided software engineering (CASE) tools improve how design decisions are documented and analyzed and the technical effort is performed. In fact, JAD may be easily tailored to dovetail with many of the development life cycles and CASE tools.

Not only is JAD a natural, evolutionary step from a software development standpoint, but it is also a logical outcome of users' involvement with computers. Users today are more eager to participate in the design process. They have become less intimidated by computers, more aware of the strategic importance of the software being developed, and frustrated by the failures of the past.

The proliferation of personal computers has helped to make users less intimidated by computers. Many users are either computer literate themselves or have computer-literate children and friends. In addition, considerable press coverage has been devoted to the strategic nature of computer systems. Users read in their own journals about the benefits of well-designed, effective software. They see such headlines as "Information Power: How Companies Are Using New Technologies to Gain a Competitive Edge" [2] and "Supporting Competitive Strategy with Information Technology: Customer Oriented Strategic Systems" [3].

The third factor explaining JAD acceptance within the user community is user frustration over past software development failures. Users shudder at the memories of spending large sums of money and waiting inordinate periods of time only to receive a system that did not meet their expectations or requirements. They remember all too well the time they spent helping to rework a delivered system, trying to make it usable. Many users realize the advantages of investing a relatively small amount of their time up front to design the system well rather than wasting considerable time and money patching a bungled system.

JAD's Expanding Uses

JAD was originally developed for use in software development projects. However, as people gain proficiency and confidence in JAD, they begin to explore other ways to reap the benefits JAD provides. JAD is now used for the following types of efforts (see Chap. 12 for further discussion):

- Defining package requirements
- Determining package modification requirements
- Designing software maintenance requests (enhancements)
- Defining office automation requirements

Although these efforts have distinct tasks and outputs, they all have the same basic JAD structure (i.e., the activities and phases described in Chaps. 2 and 3, respectively). Additionally, each of these efforts adheres to the four JAD tenets: facilitated group dynamics, visual aids, organized, structured process, and WYSIWYG documentation approach.

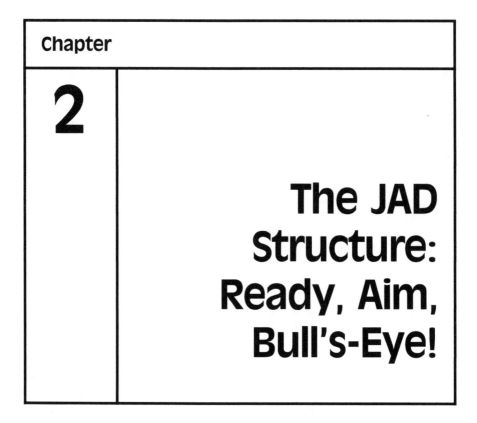

Chapter

2

The JAD Structure: Ready, Aim, Bull's-Eye!

To win his freedom the legendary archer William Tell shot an arrow and split an apple atop his son's head. What a pressured moment it must have been for Tell as he focused on his target and released the arrow, keenly aware of the threat to his son's life. As courageous and skilled a feat as William Tell accomplished, it would have been sheer lunacy had he not taken careful aim at his target. Yet software developers commonly let their design arrows fly before fully defining their targets. They rush into designing details without first obtaining a coherent concept of the overall system.

JAD AVOIDS TARGET PROBLEMS

JAD's structure and group design approach avoid the "target problems" that frequently plague software projects: divergent targets, changing or uncertain targets, outdated targets, and secret targets.

Divergent Targets

A software design project with more than one user will naturally commence with divergent targets (Fig. 2-1). Because no two people think exactly alike, users will have different ideas about what the eventual system will be. Coming from

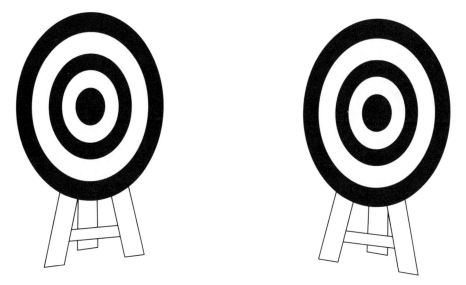

Figure 2-1   Divergent targets.

different backgrounds, each will have his or her own perspective on the general requirements for the system—the objectives, strategic and future considerations, assumptions, and constraints, to name a few—and what the system scope should encompass.

If users rush into defining the detailed requirements and design of the system, they will forfeit the opportunity to discuss, understand, and agree on a single, common target. Projects that continue with divergent targets typically incite wars within the organization. In some cases, the users battle politically among themselves over whose target will prevail. Sometimes the information systems group is called upon to impose a compromise. The individual users may not initially realize that their target has been shifted because they recognize some of its aspects in the information systems group's solution. However, sooner or later (and unfortunately it is frequently many dollars and months later), the users wake up and rebel against the imposed solution, fiercely turning against the information systems group. Such systems are often abandoned.

Changing or Uncertain Targets

Some projects suffer from targets that are constantly changing (Fig. 2-2). This is particularly symptomatic of projects whose designers neglect to develop a target fully, either because of indecision or lack of forethought. They plunge right into the design details, hoping that everything will work out in the end. As the designers get further into the design they must constantly change already designed pieces of the system in order to accommodate new design ideas. Of course these changes precipitate other changes, and so it goes.

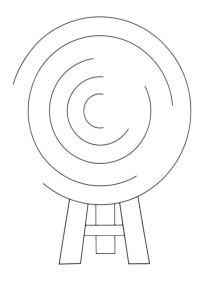

Figure 2-2   Changing or uncertain targets.

Frustration is the name of the game in such scenarios. As if on a treadmill, developers remain in a vicious cycle of designing and redesigning the system. The absence of a clearly defined target not only obscures their aim but also prevents them from evaluating the quality of each design shot.

Outdated Targets

Outdated targets (Fig. 2-3) usually imitate the organization's existing operations at the time the new system is designed. They are naturally generated by users who have limited advice or exposure to information systems. For example, if such users currently perform their work manually, they will tend to develop an image of a system that simply automates their current work process.

The relatively good news is that systems based on outdated targets frequently make it through the development cycle and are actually used. The bad news is that these systems do not provide the organization with as much "bang for the buck" as they could, for two major reasons: First, systems based on outdated targets do not allow the organization to reap all of the benefits that the technology has to offer. The idiosyncrasies and limitations imposed by the current processing methods are frequently built into the new system unnecessarily. Second, these systems frequently do not provide the organization with as much useful life as they could. Developers using outdated targets never take the opportunity to anticipate the future organizational climate. By designing the system to reflect the past, they build in system obsolescence.

Figure 2-3 Outdated targets.

Secret Targets

Secret targets (Fig. 2-4) are rarely, if ever, intentional. They are well-defined system targets that are either miscommunicated, forgotten, or simply not communicated at all. Secret targets typically come in two varieties.

The first variety occurs because a key individual—frequently the executive sponsor—concludes that there is no need to communicate his or her ideas. Sometimes the executive is reluctant to impose a solution on the other users. In other cases the executive does not make the project a high enough priority. This key individual incorrectly assumes that everyone will naturally arrive at the same system target, without his or her input.

The second type of secret target occurs when an agreed-upon system target is not adequately documented and publicized. For example, in order to justify the project funding, the user area managers may have had numerous meetings to debate and agree on the system's general requirements and scope. The agreements remain verbal or scantily documented in memos. However, as time passes and users get into the details of the design, they frequently forget or distort their initial conclusions. Furthermore, people who were not present at the original meetings are completely unaware of the decisions.

Both versions of the secret target waste system ideas. The eventual design does not and cannot accurately reflect the target that is hidden from view.

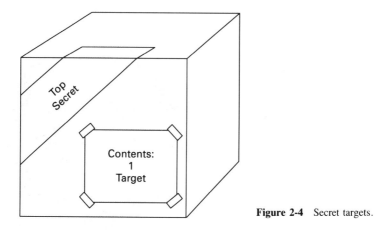

Figure 2-4   Secret targets.

JAD'S STRUCTURE ENFORCES PROJECT'S AIM

JAD's fundamental structure ensures that the right players focus as a team on the project's general requirements and scope (the bull's-eye) before they take a shot at the system details. All JAD efforts proceed through JAD's two fundamental *activities*, JAD/Plan and JAD/Design. The purpose of *JAD/Plan* is to explicitly decide on the target. Where is the bull's-eye, and how will you know when you have hit it? It addresses the objectives phase of the software development life cycle. *JAD/Design* defines the system details that bring you to your goal. This is where the requirements and external design phases are accomplished.

JAD/PLAN SETS UP THE TARGET

JAD/Plan initiates a JAD project. It draws together those user and information systems participants with a high-level, tactical perspective on the project. Guided by the session leader, they tackle the broader policy, strategic, and organizational issues. A JAD/Plan session for a small, simple project takes on the flavor of a small group meeting and is usually accomplished within a day. JAD/Plans for larger projects may affect more areas within the organization and involve up to 10 participants. The sessions for these larger JAD/Plans may last up to five days.

A JAD/Plan for a software development effort has four major objectives (see Chaps. 5 through 7 for the specific JAD/Plan tasks):

- Identify high-level system requirements.
- Define and bound the system scope.
- Plan the JAD/Design activity.
- Publish and obtain approval of the JAD/Plan document.

Identify High-Level System Requirements

In session, the JAD/Plan participants define the high-level, more global requirements for the system. They set the project direction, determining where the target should be placed. They start the JAD process off with the broader, macro issues and then refine them down to the detail level as the JAD/Plan and JAD/Design activities progress. This step-by-step, top-down approach promotes a thorough, rational analysis of the effort.

The high-level requirements typically span five topics:

- **Objectives.** What purpose should the system serve? Why are we undertaking this project?
- **Anticipated benefits.** What benefits do we expect to derive from the implementation of this system? Can these benefits be quantified (e.g., cost savings, increased revenues, efficiency, decision support)? What are the intangible benefits (e.g., job satisfaction, morale)?
- **Strategic and future considerations.** Can this system provide us with strategic advantages? What changes can be foreseen in the future operating environment of the organization (e.g., changes in the customer base, suppliers, competitors, government or legal environment, or within our own organization)? How can the system enable us to be more effective, efficient, and competitive in the future?
- **Constraints and assumptions.** Are there any constraints or assumptions for the system or the development project? Do any financial or time limitations exist? Are there any organizational or headcount constraints or assumptions? Are there specific hardware, software, or interface assumptions?
- **Security, audit, and control requirements.** What are the broad security requirements for the system? Are there audit and control points that must be considered?

Define and Bound the System Scope

When a software development project is initiated, the project scope is rarely more than a vague notion. Everyone may agree on a project name and the general areas to be covered by the system, but considerable differences of opinion may exist over the scope specifics. For example, all individuals within an organization may agree that what is needed is a sales support system covering order processing and sales management. They may even have come up with a system name with a flashy acronym—Sales Processing and Reporting (SUPER). However, individuals may hold differing opinions on the specific scope areas. Should the system perform an automatic customer credit check? Should the system support the entire sales force appraisal process, or should it be limited to the tracking and analysis of sales achievement versus quota?

During the JAD/Plan group session, participants clearly and succinctly define the overall scope of the project. This is where they agree on the target's bull's-eye and paint it red for all to see. They reference the high-level requirements to ensure that the scope will meet the organization's needs. Rather than sweeping policy issues under the rug, the group confronts them head-on, generating ideas, sharing opinions, and deciding on solutions. Together, the participants draw a boundary around the system, identifying the functional areas that fall inside the system scope and those that are excluded.

Plan the JAD/Design Activity

Once the JAD/Plan participants define the overall system, they develop a plan to accomplish the design of the scope through JAD/Designs. The plan includes time estimates and staffing commitments, as well as a schedule of project milestones.

In order to develop the plan, the session leader must first estimate how long it will take to design the defined scope. If the overall scope is small to medium—that is, following the estimation guidelines outlined in Chap. 6, it can be designed within 10 days of group sessions—one JAD/Design can address the entire scope. For larger systems, the overall scope is broken down into manageable topics for individual JAD/Designs. In such cases, a single JAD/Plan addressing the entire system would be followed by two or more JAD/Designs, to be performed sequentially. Each JAD/Design would be like a piece of a puzzle, covering a well-defined subsystem, or logically related piece of the overall system scope (see Fig. 2-5). Once estimation of the JAD/Designs has been completed, the appropriate

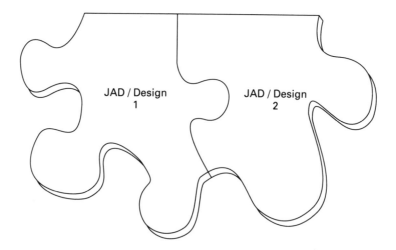

Figure 2-5   Subsystems for JAD/Designs. The JAD/Design subsystems are like pieces of a puzzle that together make up the system scope.

participants for the JAD/Designs are identified and a commitment is made for their availability. The JAD/Designs are then sequenced and scheduled, taking into account major conflicts such as holidays, year-end closings, and important organizational events. After all, group dynamics will be of little use if a session is scheduled for New Year's Day.

Publish and Obtain Approval of the JAD/Plan Document

No matter how creative and enlightening a group session is, most of the work will have been for nought if the results are not documented clearly and completely, formally approved by the project's executive sponsor, and distributed to the JAD/Plan and JAD/Design participants. Consensus among the JAD/Plan participants may have been reached during the session. But unless the results of the session are documented, as time passes people may forget or have different recollections of what was decided. Thorough documentation of the results avoids having to rehash the issues later on. It also helps to inform those individuals who were not JAD/Plan participants of the decisions made during the session.

Once the JAD/Plan results are documented, the JAD/Plan participants review the output to ensure that it accurately and thoroughly reflects the session results. The executive sponsor—that individual with "go/no-go" decision-making authority over the project—should then be required to approve the results formally. This practice serves two purposes. First, the required sign-off adds responsibility and weight to both the document review and the document's validity and credibility. Second, formal approval is a valuable project management mechanism. You now have a project baseline or foundation that bounds the effort; nothing can become part of the project baseline unless its impact on the project has been analyzed and the change has received a formal executive approval.

The approved document is then distributed to the JAD/Plan participants as well as to all of the designated JAD/Design participants. The JAD/Plan document now serves as a communications tool and reference guide. Those individuals chosen to participate in the upcoming JAD/Design(s) will know when they are expected to be present for the sessions. They will also be able to read about the high-level requirements and the scope of the system that they will be designing in more detail.

JAD/DESIGN HITS THE BULL'S-EYE

During JAD/Design, the participants aim at the JAD/Plan target, shoot their design arrows, and hit a bull's-eye. Guided by the JAD/Plan document, the participants create the users' view of the system, the requirements and external design. They decide exactly what they want the system to do and display. Although the JAD/Design captures the information needed to perform the technical development tasks (i.e., database and program design, coding and testing), it stops short of actually accomplishing them. These tasks will be performed subsequent to the JAD effort by a technical team.

Whereas the JAD/Plan participants are selected from the higher ranks of the organization, the JAD/Design participants are typically a more mixed group. They directly reflect the levels and departments of the organization that the system will serve. Within the JAD/Design forum, individuals ranging from chairman of the board to data entry operator may share ideas and gain a better understanding of the areas addressed by the system. In addition, the information systems representative provides software design expertise and advice to the users.

A JAD/Design for a software development effort has four major objectives (see Chaps. 8 through 10 for the specific JAD/Design tasks):

- Define detailed requirements and scope.
- Design screen and report layouts.
- Capture edit, validation, processing, and interface requirements.
- Develop the prototype.
- Complete and obtain approval of the JAD/Design document.

Define Detailed Requirements and Scope

The high-level requirements gathered during the JAD/Plan provide the basis for the JAD/Design. During the JAD/Design group session, participants refine and provide greater details about the requirements. They also define how work will be accomplished once the new system is in place.

The focus of the discussion is on how the organization should operate in the future. Participants are urged to improve the current environment, not simply automate it. They manipulate JAD magnetics in order to diagram and more effectively envision the various system alternatives. They cross-educate each other, sharing problems, concerns, and ideas for improvements. The diagram and its supporting text help participants to define more effectively how the system will support the organization.

Design Screen and Report Layouts

The JAD/Design participants examine the requirements and identify which screens and reports are needed for the new system. For each screen and report on the design list, participants decide which data elements should be included on the layout.

The first time a data element is mentioned for inclusion in the system, time is taken to capture relevant information. Participants define the data element's meaning and provide other information such as its size and data type. Participants then begin the fun and creative process of designing the layout. They learn about and discuss screen and report design considerations in order to better understand their trade-offs (e.g., crowding versus paging). They move JAD data element magnetics around, determining where each one should be placed to create the most effective screen or report.

Capture Edit, Validation, Processing, and Interface Requirements

For each screen designed, participants determine what supporting editing and validation the system must perform. For example, on the "Add an Order" screen, should the system ensure that the customer number entered is already on file? Should the customer's standard billing address be modifiable for a single order? Where appropriate, processing requirements also are specified. These may vary from simple screen or report calculations to major processing routines.

Additionally, participants define the requirements for passing data between systems, called system interfaces. This is not a technical interface design. Like everything else in JAD, it is a user-oriented specification. Participants identify the direction of the interface (from which system to which system), the frequency of the interface, and the data elements to be passed.

Develop the Prototype

The design generated in session is validated through the use of a prototype. (A prototype is analogous to a Hollywood set whose buildings have very real looking façades but lack foundations, roofs, or major internal systems such as plumbing and heating.) The prototype screen layouts appear on the computer screen and may even have much of the edit and validation logic to demonstrate. Many prototyping environments make it easy to add navigation to the prototype, so that you can see how to go from a menu selection to the screen function and back to the menu. If the prototyping and implementation environments are compatible, the prototype does not even have to be a separate "throwaway" effort; design and development of the final system can continue where the prototype leaves off.

Validates the design. A prototype provides an excellent vehicle to validate the design further before making the comparatively large dollar and time investment in implementing the full-scale system. The tangible look and feel of the system come across to users of a prototype much more vividly than a mere picture of a screen.

Educates and communicates. In addition to validating the design, the prototype can be used as an education and communications tool. It can be an extremely effective way to demonstrate the system to the executive sponsor and anyone else who did not participate directly in the JAD/Design sessions. For example, when new members on the technical team begin the project, they will have to learn about the system they will be building. Certainly the JAD/Design document will be their authoritative guide to the details of the system. However, what better way to introduce them to the system than to have them run through the prototype.

Complete and Obtain Approval of the JAD/Design Document

Complete the JAD/Design document.   The JAD/Design session results are formally recorded in the JAD/Design document. The document is written for both user and technical team consumption. The user community must be able to review, understand, and analyze the documented design as a quality assurance measure. The technical team must be able to build the system from the JAD/Design document specifications.

On traditional software development projects, where the information systems department interviews users separately and then writes the requirements and external design documents for the project, obtaining a thorough user review of the document is a rare occurrence. The documents are long, and the users, pressed for time by the normal demands of their jobs, generally read the "mom and apple pie" introductions and skim through the remaining, meatier sections. By contrast, the JAD users comb the document to ensure its accuracy. Two major factors account for this difference: ease of review and document ownership.

Ease of document review.   In JAD, both the format and the content of the document are familiar to the participant reviewers. The JAD/Design document format reflects the visual aids used within the JAD/Design group session—what you see is what you get. In addition, all of the participants were present for the discussions and decisions. This avoids the fragmented understanding of the system a user might get after having been one interviewee in a series of interviews performed by the technical team. The JAD user participants therefore are able to bring to the review a thorough understanding of the entire system design, as opposed to the traditional user participants who must rely solely on the discussion that occurred during their interviews.

Document ownership.   Document ownership also plays a major role in obtaining effective user review of the document. All of the participants designed the system as a team. If any finger pointing is ever done, the entire team is under indictment. This increases the feeling of responsibility for a high-quality output.

Executive approval.   As in the case of the JAD/Plan document, the reviewed JAD/Design document is formally approved by the executive sponsor. The JAD/Design participants make a formal presentation of the system to the executive sponsor, as well as providing him or her with a copy of the document. The executive approval explicitly incorporates the JAD/Design document into the project baseline or foundation, helping management to track and control the system development effort.

HOW MUCH IS ENOUGH USER INVOLVEMENT?

Software developers continually debate the question, How far into the design process should you ask the users to go? How much user involvement is enough? Other software design methodologies stop user involvement after data elements have been identified for screens and reports. Under these methodologies, screen and report layout designs are the sole province of the information systems professionals. With JAD, users' involvement is expanded dramatically. Users are asked to design the complete external design—the entire users' view of the system. JAD's reasons are both pragmatic and philosophical.

First, for the pragmatic view: Designing the layouts is one of the more rewarding, less time-consuming, and more important efforts for users to accomplish. Moving data element magnetics around in order to design a screen or report is a creative, fun task. It is not particularly time consuming once you have identified all the data elements that belong on the screen or report. In fact, as they manipulate the data elements and further discuss the layout, participants often alter and improve their initial list of data elements. However, the most significant benefit of having users design their own screen and report layouts is that in doing so they solidify their commitment to the system. You are enabling them to provide tangible input into the design; when they see the layouts in the prototype, JAD/Design document, and eventual system, they recognize those layouts as their own.

Personally, I am totally convinced by the pragmatic view. But for the philosophers among us, there is a simple theoretical basis for keeping users involved. The more theoretical argument holds that the users' view of the system should be designed by the users. It is not technical knowledge of computers that drives the external design. Rather, the external design is fueled by in-depth understanding of the organization's operations and the nuances of intended system use. Who better understands how the system will be used than the users themselves?

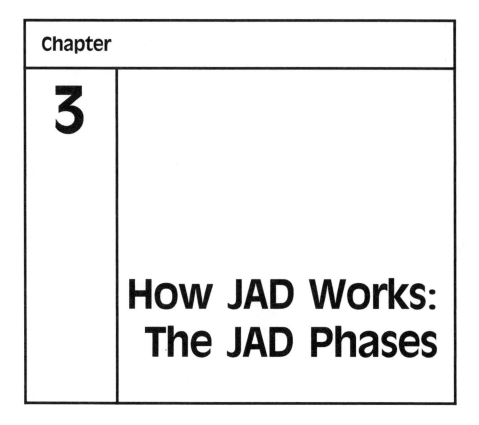

Chapter

3

How JAD Works: The JAD Phases

A complex effort is more easily learned and accomplished when its many tasks are grouped into logically related units or phases. For example, the activity of having a meal, so much enjoyed and well practiced by many of us, may be divided into the three phases of preparation, eating, and cleanup. Regardless of the specific meal, or whether you are cooking and eating in, bringing in, or eating out, you will always have some preparation (e.g., baking at 350 degrees, calling for take-out, ordering from a menu), eating, and cleanup tasks.

Just as in the example of having a meal, so any JAD is divided into logically related phases: customization, session, and wrap-up. Regardless of whether you are performing the JAD/Plan or JAD/Design activity, or whether the JAD effort is aimed at software development, package specifications, or office automation re-quirements (see Chap. 12 for JAD's expanded uses), there will always be some customization, session, and wrap-up tasks. Each of the three JAD phases takes on its own character, with typical participants and objectives.

- **Customization** is the first phase performed in any JAD and is largely composed of preparation tasks for the session phase to come. The major participants in this phase are the session leader and one or two JAD analysts. Typically, customization requires 1 to 10 days.

- **Session** is the "meat" of the JAD. It consists of facilitated group sessions, where users and information systems representatives jointly develop the requirements and/or design of the system. The session leader facilitates the group dynamics and leads the participants through the session tasks, and the analyst documents the session results. This phase typically lasts 1 to 10 days.

- **Wrap-Up** is the final JAD phase. Its tasks revolve around producing the formal JAD outputs. The session leader and analyst transform the session visual aids and handwritten forms into the JAD document. The JAD/Design results are also prototyped and presented to the executive sponsor. The wrap-up phase typically requires 3 to 15 days.

HOW DO THE PHASES FIT TOGETHER?

To continue the meal analogy, just as some clean-up tasks may be accomplished along with the preparation and eating tasks, so in JAD some of the wrap-up tasks may be performed with the session tasks. In fact, a frequently desirable planning alternative is to schedule part-time sessions, such as half days or three days a week. Wrap-up then fills in the nonsession calendar time and allows users to attend to the more pressing matters of their usual jobs (Chap. 6 discusses JAD scheduling in more depth).

Since the three phases apply to all JADs, any given effort will consist of a repeating series of customization, session, and wrap-up. Figure 3-1 illustrates the

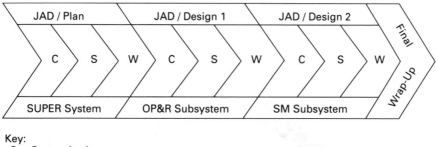

Key:
C = Customization
S = Session
W = Wrap-up

Figure 3-1   JAD structure for SUPER system. The JAD/Plan is followed by two JAD/Designs, performed sequentially. The JAD/Plan and two JAD/Designs are each composed of the three JAD phases: customization, session, and wrap-up.

JAD structure for the software development effort to design the Sales Processing and Reporting (SUPER) system. The project starts with the customization, session, and wrap-up phases for a JAD/Plan. During the JAD/Plan session phase, the participants define the need for a JAD/Design for order processing and reporting (OP&R) followed by a second JAD/Design for sales management (SM)—assigning, tracking, and evaluating sales force quotas versus achievements. Each of the two JAD/Designs has its own sequence of customization, session, and wrap-up phases.

When a project has more than one JAD/Design activity, final wrap-up time is allotted at the conclusion of all of the JAD/Designs. This time is used for final review of the design as a whole. In the SUPER system example, the session leader adds final wrap-up time at the conclusion of the sales management JAD/Design. The JAD participants use this time to examine the "seams" between subsystems. Their goal is to ensure that the subsystems fit together smoothly as originally envisioned during the JAD/Plan session.

CUSTOMIZATION FOR SOFTWARE DESIGN

If preparation is the key to success, customization is the key to an effective JAD for software design (Fig. 3-2). The session leader and one or two JAD analysts do most of the preparation for the JAD/Plan and JAD/Design activities of a software design effort. The managers, users, and information systems personnel selected as participants for the next session phase are involved minimally during customization, on an as-needed basis only. Although the specific customization tasks differ somewhat for the JAD/Plan and JAD/Design activities, four categories of tasks are accomplished:

- Conduct orientation.
- Organize JAD team.
- Tailor JAD tasks and outputs.
- Prepare materials for session.

Conduct Orientation: Scouting Out the Project

During the orientation tasks, the session leader and analyst(s) familiarize themselves with the area to be addressed in session. This is not an in-depth requirements analysis, by any means; you do not want to duplicate the session effort. Rather, the goal here is to gain a broad understanding of the JAD's functional area, people, and terminology. As a session leader familiarizing myself with the area to be addressed by the JAD, I always try to scout out where the potential session stumbling blocks lie. What are the project complexities? What are some of the major decisions with which the participants may have to grapple?

In addition, the session leader and analyst(s) try to uncover any issues or considerations that may affect the upcoming JAD/Plan or JAD/Design session. In

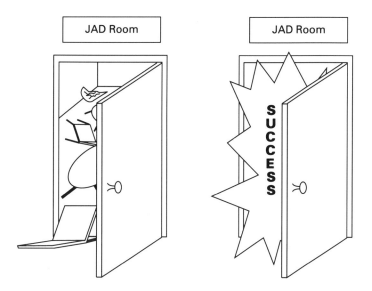

Figure 3-2   Customization. The difference between a disorganized session and a professional, well-run session is often due to customization.

JAD, "issue" and "consideration" have specialized meanings. An *issue* is an item that pertains to the session scope but cannot be resolved by the participants because they lack either information or authority. When the session leader uncovers a potential issue during customization, he or she tries to obtain a resolution before the session starts. This may involve presenting the issue to the executive sponsor for his or her decision or asking a participant to obtain information on a certain topic and present it during the session.

For example, during customization for the order processing and reporting JAD/Design, the session leader may discover that the pricing algorithms are fairly complex. Anticipating that none of the session participants would be able to recite the algorithms off the top of their head, the session leader may ask the appropriate user representative to develop a transparency describing the pricing algorithms. The user would then review the transparency with the other participants at the appropriate time in session.

Consideration refers to an item that arises in session but is outside the scope of the current session. A consideration may either affect another JAD session, the technical effort, a subsequent release or version of the system, or the business in general. The key aspect of a consideration is that the idea has potential value to the organization. JAD documents considerations for later review and analysis. This avoids having either to discard the idea because it is outside the session scope or fully discuss the idea then and there and going off on a tangent.

During JAD/Design customization, the session leader and analyst(s) review the considerations that arose during earlier JADs. An item affecting the current

JAD/Design may have arisen and been documented as a consideration during the JAD/Plan or, in the case of a multi-JAD/Design system, during a prior JAD/Design. The session leader and analyst(s) review these considerations and incorporate them in appropriate places within the current session agenda.

Organize the Team: Avoiding the Missing Person

No one thinks it could ever happen. The visual aids are ready, the room is set up, the coffee and Danish have arrived. Yes, today is the first day of session. But where are the participants?

It is the responsibility of the session leader and executive sponsor to organize the participants. The goal of this task category is to ensure that the appropriate participants will attend the session and that they come to the session prepared. In the case of JAD/Plan customization, the participants for the session phase may or may not have been selected before the session leader becomes involved in the project. If the participants have not been named, the session leader will help the executive sponsor to determine who should attend the session. If, on the other hand, the participants have already been chosen, the session leader will help to confirm that no one was inadvertently omitted from the participant list.

The participants for the JAD/Design session are selected during the JAD/Plan session phase and recorded in the JAD/Plan document. Many session leaders fall into the trap of assuming that the participant selection process is thus complete. They forget that we live in a rapidly changing world, one in which such events as promotions, transfers, reorganizations, and resignations happen overnight. During customization for any given JAD/Design, the session leader confirms with management that the original participant list remains appropriate.

After the participant list is confirmed, the session leader ensures that the participants come to the session prepared. This involves communicating session logistics to all of the participants (dates, times, and place of the sessions) and providing JAD background. The JAD background includes an overview of the JAD methodology along with an explanation of how each type of participant (executive, user, information systems personnel) should prepare for the session. If the JAD analysts are new to the methodology, they must receive in-depth training in JAD. For JAD/Designs, the session leader ensures that all participants have received the JAD/Plan document as well.

Tailor JAD: Obtaining a Perfect Project Fit

JAD stands out among methodologies in the way that it encourages the session leader to tailor the standard tasks and formats both to the organization and to the idiosyncrasies of the specific project underway. The goal is to provide the best fit for the situation at hand. For example, an organization may want to continue to use a documentation software tool that imposes some of its own standards (e.g., the use of data flow diagrams instead of workflow diagrams). An experienced session leader examines such considerations and devises ways to compensate for them within the JAD framework. In doing so, the session leader must be careful to maintain the major JAD tenets:

- The facilitated group session approach
- Effective use of visual aids to illustrate objectives, requirements, and design
- Organized, rational process
- What you see in session is what you get documentation approach

The session leader performs most of the JAD tailoring during customization for the JAD/Plan. This will enable him or her to develop more accurate task-by-task estimates of the JAD/Designs (to be estimated during the JAD/Plan session), as well as confirm the estimates for the remaining JAD/Plan phases. Most of the tailoring occurs the first time the organization performs a JAD and any time the organization implements a major change in standards. However, the session leader may find it necessary to make minor changes to the process and formats during the customization phase for any JAD/Plan or JAD/Design.

Prepare Materials: Get Ready, Get Set

Preparing the session phase materials is one of the more time-consuming sets of tasks that the session leader and analyst(s) perform during customization. It encompasses arranging for the room, equipment, and materials; preparing the many visual aids; laying the groundwork for the documentation effort; and setting up the session room.

Arrange for the room, equipment, and materials.   The session leader and analyst(s) coordinate with the appropriate personnel to arrange for a Session room, visual aid equipment, and materials. The decision must be made as to whether or not to hold the session off-site (e.g., in a hotel or another organization-owned facility). The advantage in holding the session off-site is that the participants are less likely to be interrupted or distracted by the continuing demands of their jobs. Of course, budgetary constraints also affect this decision.

Prepare visual aids.   The session leader and analyst(s) use the equipment and materials to prepare two types of visual aids. They develop informative visuals that will help to communicate already known information about the project and JAD to the session participants. They also develop preformatted visuals (forms) that will be completed during the session.

Set up documentation environment.   Customization is also when the analyst(s) lay the groundwork for the documentation effort. They create a skeleton document online that contains all of the JAD forms and formats. This speeds the documentation effort by allowing the analyst(s) merely to "fill in the blanks" with the session results. It also helps to ensure documentation consistency, as each form is a copy of the original. The analyst(s) develop naming conventions for each of the forms to expedite data entry and retrieval. Together with the session leader, they plan the note-taking and documentation effort (who does what and when).

Set up session room. The day before the session phase begins, the session leader and analyst(s) set up the session room. They must arrange the seating, hang the flip charts, and set up the overhead and/or slide projector, magnetic board, and the automated documentation system (if used). Seating is typically around a conference table or in a horseshoe arrangement of tables, depending on the size and shape of the room and the number of participants. A good seating arrangement promotes open discussions, and the visual aids will provide the participants with readily accessible reference points and mind joggers during the session phase.

SESSION FOR SOFTWARE DESIGN

The actual process of ascertaining system objectives and requirements and creating the external design (the users' view of the system) occurs during the session phase. JAD harnesses group dynamics to generate ideas and make decisions that result in innovative, synergistic solutions (Fig. 3-3).

Figure 3-3 Session. During the session, one idea builds on the next as people from different areas within the organization listen to each other's views and concerns.

During the session phase, the "right" people interact in a group session environment in order to better understand, evaluate, define the requirements for, and design the system. It is this group session approach that truly sets JAD apart from other design methodologies and injects such a large dose of creativity and innovation into the design process. The session leader facilitates the process, guiding representatives from the user and information systems groups through the structured JAD tasks. The JAD analyst(s) help to track and record the effort and may also provide input into the discussions. The executive sponsor participates in the JAD/Plan session to help determine the high-level requirements; he or she may also be involved sporadically during the JAD/Design sessions.

The group session approach is a highly effective and productive way to gather the requirements and to design a system, particularly when compared to other approaches. Using more traditional methods, systems analysts go through the lengthy process of trying to learn the users' functions through one-on-one or small group interviews. They then try to digest what they have heard and resolve any discrepancies or conflicts that they detected in the interviews. As if that wasn't challenging enough, during the external design phase of the effort, systems analysts are required to second-guess the users. They have to synthesize what they learned about the users' jobs in order to design the screens, reports, and processing for the system. With such a tall order, it's no wonder that users are rarely completely satisfied with the resulting design.

JAD improves the traditional approach by including both experienced users and information systems professionals on the design team. The systems analysts no longer have to go through the lengthy and often futile process of trying to master the users' knowledge and experience in order to second-guess what the users want in a system. The users bring to the table their knowledge of intricacies, exceptions, and strategic considerations. They are encouraged to generate new ideas and to discuss openly with other users and information systems professionals their ideas for improvements. Naturally, this will result in a higher quality, more innovative system design.

For any given task, the JAD session format follows a typical pattern, consisting of four steps (see Chap. 11 for additional information):

- Task presentation
- Idea generation
- Evaluation
- Commitment

Task Presentation

It's the session leader's nightmare: being in front of the session room, asking the participants to begin a discussion, and receiving silent, blank stares in return. Anxiety sets in as eyebrows furrow and the expressions on people's faces become increasingly perplexed.

One of the most important factors in generating meaningful, lively discussions is to clearly present the task at hand. In JAD, the session leader initiates each task by explaining to the participants what they are to accomplish. He or she may provide sample outputs (a sample workflow diagram, e.g.) or may make a formal presentation on the topic. When a type of task is performed repetitively, as when designing many screen layouts for the system, the session leader provides the detailed explanation for the first occurrence. Subsequently, he or she defines what is to be done ("We are now going to design the Add an Order screen") and may remind the participants of some of the initial material presented on the topic ("Remember that you will probably want to place toward the top of the screen those fields required on data entry").

Idea Generation

After the session leader defines the current task, the participants offer their ideas on the topic. This is a time for creativity and innovation as the participants discuss various alternative solutions. When conflicting opinions arise, the session leader encourages the participants to develop new, synergistic solutions that draw on the advantages of those ideas previously offered. One idea frequently sparks another as people from different areas within the organization listen to each other's views and concerns. The session leader ensures that the discussion stays within the scope of the JAD and on the current topic.

Evaluation

The participants then decide if they have found a good solution for the current task or more ideas must be generated. Is the solution consistent with previously made decisions? Will it satisfy all user groups? Is it a sound, implementable information systems idea? The session leader helps the participants to reach a consensus for a solution.

Commitment

When the session participants come to an agreement, the session leader summarizes the solution and either the session leader or the analyst records it. This solution then becomes one developed and owned by the entire group. It is built on all of the participants' ideas, concerns, and expertise. They agree to and become committed to the design as a team.

WRAP-UP FOR SOFTWARE DESIGN

During the wrap-up phase, the formal JAD outputs are produced. The handwritten session visual aids and forms are transformed into a JAD/Plan or JAD/Design document. Additionally, in the case of JAD/Design, a prototype is built, and the design results are formally presented to the executive sponsor (Fig. 3-4).

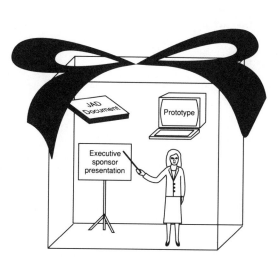

Figure 3-4   Wrap-up. During wrap-up the session visual aids and forms are repackaged into the formal JAD outputs.

Samples of the JAD/Plan and JAD/Design document table of contents are found in Appendix C and Appendix D, respectively. These documents directly reflect the decisions and formats generated during the session. The session leader and analyst(s) add a document introduction, as well as section introductions, in order to ease the review process for readers not involved in the session. The completed document is distributed to the session participants, who review it for accuracy, clarity, and completeness. Any necessary updates are made and executive sign-off is obtained. The final JAD/Plan document is distributed to all JAD/Plan and JAD/Design participants. The final JAD/Design document is distributed to the JAD/Design participants and executive sponsor. It will also be distributed and used extensively by the technical team to develop the technical, internal design of the system.

A prototype is a second output produced during the JAD/Design wrap-up phase. A prototype is a model system, developed to make the design more tangible and more effectively reviewed. It usually includes all of the screen layouts designed during the session phase and may include sample processing and navigation as well. It is usually developed by the information systems representative from the JAD/Design session.

The final output of the JAD/Design wrap-up phase is a presentation of the system design to the executive sponsor. During the JAD/Design, the executive sponsor does not typically participate in the entire session phase. Therefore, this is a way for the users to report back to the executive sponsor and explain the session results. They may use the prototype as a visual aid in order to demonstrate the system's capabilities and its look and feel. The executive sponsor's approval will be sought before subsequent phases of the development cycle.

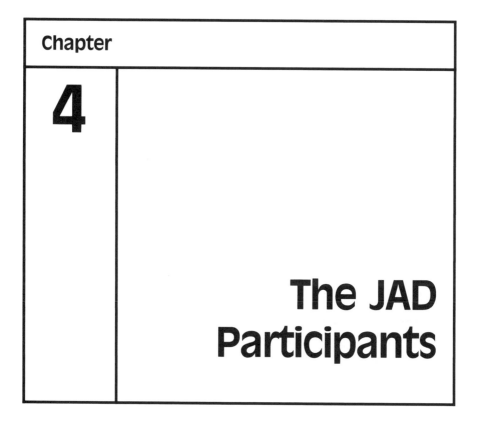

Chapter

4

The JAD Participants

The participants occupy center stage in JAD. They are the stars who have the power to make or break the performance. If the people selected to design the system are inexperienced in their jobs, unimaginative and resistant to change, the resulting system design will not fully serve the organization's needs. Given the organization's best and brightest, the JAD methodology will produce highly effective, innovative solutions.

In fact, the JAD process is an organization's opportunity to leverage its top performers (Fig. 4-1). Although the results of the JAD have a tremendous impact on the usefulness and success of the eventual system, the amount of participant time and money that an organization invests in the JAD is small relative to the time and cost of the entire software development effort. Even so, the real payoff for the organization occurs when the system goes into operation. All of the system's users now have access to a software resource that reflects the knowledge and creativity of the organization's finest.

WHAT ARE THE JAD PARTICIPANT ROLES?

The individuals assigned to a JAD have unique roles that they play. JAD defines six different types of participants (see Fig. 4-2). A JAD role does not necessarily translate into a single person; an individual may perform more than one role, and a

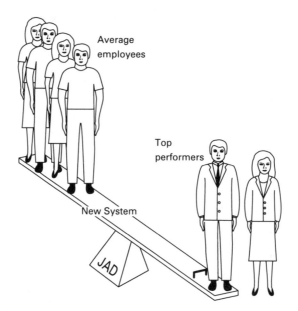

Figure 4-1 JAD enables an organization to leverage the knowledge and creativity of its top performers.

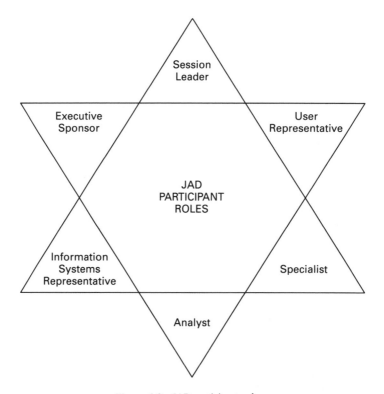

Figure 4-2 JAD participant roles.

role may be filled by more than one individual. For example, a person may simultaneously be the executive sponsor and user representative if he or she has ultimate authority over the project and is also a major user of the system. A typical example of a role filled by a number of people is the case of the user representative, where many individuals are typically needed to provide the users' perspective.

HOW MANY PARTICIPANTS?

Although the number of participants will vary considerably, depending on the size and nature of the system being designed, no more than 15 people should be in the session room at the same time. The best of session leaders cannot possibly manage more than 15 participants effectively.

In an ideal session, everyone's attention is focused on a certain topic, with one participant's views being aired at a time. Everyone hears what is being said and has the opportunity to react. However, in excessively large sessions, the number of people who want to express their ideas at any given time is so great that the participants naturally form splinter groups. Rather than waiting for the chance to explain their ideas to the whole session, people discuss their opinions with the participants sitting near them. In doing so, they miss what is being said in session, and the other participants miss what they are saying privately. The room takes on the air of a three-ring circus.

A two-person session may be appropriate for a JAD/Plan focusing on a small system. In this case, the executive sponsor may be able to provide most if not all of the high-level information required. The extreme of a 15-person session may be appropriate for a fairly large and complex JAD/Design that affects a number of different user disciplines. However, a more typical number of JAD participants lies somewhere between the two extremes.

WHAT ABOUT OBSERVERS?

Occasionally, in trying to keep the official number of session participants within the appropriate range, an organization will attempt to create the role of "user or information systems observer." Individuals chosen for this role are told to attend the session and listen to the discussions, but to remain silent. This arrangement rarely, if ever, succeeds. The discussions become so lively and exciting that the observers find it irresistible to contribute their ideas. In one instance, the observers became so frustrated that they wrote down their ideas and flew them on paper airplanes for the "official" participants to contribute for them.

HOW ARE THE PARTICIPANTS SELECTED?

Prior to or during JAD/Plan customization, the session leader usually assists the executive sponsor in selecting the individuals who will fill the other JAD/Plan roles. The JAD/Plan participants then identify the JAD/Design participants during the JAD/Plan session phase. In deciding which individuals are most qualified to

participate in the JAD, job experience, industry knowledge, and personal characteristics should all be considered.

SESSION LEADER

The session leader is the orchestra conductor who brings the various JAD participants together and inspires them to work in harmony. The session leader does not
define the requirements or design the system, but rather sets the stage for the JAD
and leads the other participants through the process. His or her primary responsibilities are to organize the JAD, facilitate group dynamics, and provide JAD
expertise. The session leader participates in all phases of the JAD. During customization, he or she becomes oriented to the project, organizes the JAD team, tailors
the JAD process and outputs, and prepares the session phase materials. The session
leader is usually responsible for estimating, planning, and tracking all of the
specific tasks as well.

The session leader's skills are really put to the test during the session phase of
the JAD. It is here that a session leader's in-depth knowledge of the JAD methodology, superb facilitation skills, and quick thinking capabilities can make or break a
JAD. A session could be thrown off track if the session leader does not understand
the methodology thoroughly enough to explain it to the participants and get them
involved. The participants should never be left dumbfounded, looking at each other
and wondering exactly what they are supposed to do and why. The session leader
must have enough JAD knowledge, experience, and tools to be able to effectively
represent the methodology to the group.

Effective facilitation skills have kept many a session from complete disin-
tegration. In order to facilitate group dynamics, the session leader must be able to
manage the discussion and overcome the people issues that inevitably arise (see
Chap. 11). How do you get a discussion going? How do you keep it on track until its
conclusion? How do you diagnose an interpersonal problem? What alternatives are
available for addressing the problems? The session leader is constantly considering
and responding to all of these issues as the session progresses. During wrap-up, the
session leader works with the participants in developing the executive sponsor
presentation. He or she may also help to complete the formal JAD outputs (i.e., the
document and prototype).

When choosing individuals to be trained as session leaders, excellent interpersonal skills should be a top priority. These are skills that are more difficult to teach
than some of the other desirable traits, such as presentation, writing, and facilitation
skills. Session leaders should be energetic people who can stay enthusiastic during
sometimes long and strenuous meetings. A good sense of humor comes in handy to
release tension and relieve some of the fatigue that can set in on a particularly
demanding session day when problematic stumbling blocks call for large doses of
participant creativity. A session leader must be a person who at all times is ready for
the curve ball, constantly willing to expect the unexpected.

Session leaders must have JAD expertise, both in theory and in practice. Also essential is an application development background in order to understand fully the ultimate purpose of each of the JAD tasks and outputs. This will also make the session leader more effective in tailoring the JAD to the specific project during the customization phase. Session leaders should be responsible, well-organized individuals who can plan and track the many tasks necessary to accomplish the JAD effort.

ANALYST

The analyst has primary responsibility for producing the JAD output documents. As innovative and productive as the session may be, it will only be truly effective if the results are well documented for further use. In addition to recording the session results, the analyst may contribute his or her own ideas to the session discussions, assist and support the session leader, and develop the prototype. Analysts may also become key players in performing the technical work that follows the JAD effort. The project may be staffed with either one or two analysts, depending on how extensive the documentation effort is and how quickly the document is to be completed.

The analyst participates full time in all of the JAD phases. During customization, he or she sets up the documentation environment and organizes the entire note-taking and documentation effort. He or she may also work with the session leader on the orientation, tailoring, and materials preparation tasks. During the session phase, the analyst helps to record the design decisions either manually (by taking notes) or on an automated system, sometimes contributing ideas to the discussions as well. Wrap-up is when the analyst completes the formal documentation effort and may also develop a prototype of the system design.

Many people are fooled into thinking that the analyst's role may be staffed with clerical personnel.[1] In doing so, they discover that they have created a fiasco for themselves, as the session is continually slowed down by the need to explain to the analyst what should be recorded and on which form. To be effective, the analyst must be trained in JAD and its formats, must be competent on the documentation system, and must be able to follow and understand the session discussion. Analysts must be well organized and responsible individuals and should have good communications skills. If they are to develop the prototype, they should also have experience with the prototype software.

The role of analyst is typically staffed with systems analysts or programmers. One successful strategy is to fill the analyst role with an individual who is intended to participate in the follow-on phases once the JAD work is completed. This reduces or eliminates the need for a transition stage where the JAD results are handed over to new follow-on technical players. The analyst role is also frequently used as a training ground for prospective session leaders. They learn the JAD forms, witness

---

[1] When JAD was originated, the role now called "analyst" was called "scribe." The terminology itself misled many people into believing that the position was merely clerical.

a JAD as it progresses, and have the opportunity to assist the session leader in some of the session leader tasks and presentations.

EXECUTIVE SPONSOR

The executive sponsor has the ultimate responsibility and authority over the functional area that the system is to address. The executive sponsor is typically a high-level manager within the user community who controls the funding and user staffing for the project.

The executive sponsor has two major purposes within the JAD context. The first purpose is to impart high-level, strategic insight to the other participants. Ideally, there is perfect communication within an organization and all of the users fully understand where the organization, industry, and competition are going. In fact, such is rarely the case. This is one of the reasons why many new systems are merely slight variations on the current environment. The JAD methodology elicits this high-level, strategic information from the executive sponsor and his or her management team and communicates it to all of the JAD participants. This broad perspective is incorporated into the design, generating a more future-oriented, innovative system.

The second purpose is to make decisions and commitments that are consistent with the organization's goals and constraints. The executive sponsor must sign off on each of the JAD outputs and formally approve any changes in decisions made previously. During the course of a JAD/Design, the participants may call on the executive sponsor to resolve a JAD issue that they do not have the authority to resolve themselves. In addition, it is the executive sponsor's responsibility to keep the project staffed and funded into the production stage, when the system becomes an organizational asset.

The executive sponsor participates full time during the relatively short JAD/Plan session phase and sporadically throughout the remaining JAD/Plan and JAD/Design phases. During the JAD/Plan session phase, the executive sponsor helps to lay the groundwork for the system, determining the high-level requirements, specifying the project scope, and planning future JAD/Design activity. During the remainder of the JAD, the executive sponsor may be asked to resolve JAD issues and authorize requests for changes that arise. He or she is also the focal point of the executive sponsor presentation during JAD/Design wrap-up, and reviews and formally approves the JAD documents.

An effective executive sponsor has full authority over the project, is a good decision maker, and has a thorough understanding of the broad picture. He or she need not be a master of operational details, but must have competent, reliable associates and subordinates to consult whenever the need arises.

USER REPRESENTATIVE

The user representative is the main focus of the JAD. Jointly with the other participants, he or she examines the organization's information processing needs and generates new approaches to address the defined requirements. Each user representative brings expertise in a specific area of the organization, the willingness to learn about other disciplines, and the creativity to synthesize the information in order to design an effective system.

The interaction of the user representatives among themselves and with the other participants is what enables JAD to create such unique, innovative solutions. All too often an organization wastes its resources on antiquated reports and convoluted or inappropriate procedures simply because the organization is too compartmentalized to realize that these procedures are no longer useful. One department may spend considerable time preparing a completely unnecessary report for another department without realizing that it could be done a better way or eliminated altogether. By enabling the user representatives to learn more about each other's responsibilities, problems, and concerns, the JAD enables them to make better design decisions.

During JAD/Plan, the user representatives are higher level managers and key employees within the organization. These are individuals who can provide valuable input into the high-level requirements, system scope, and JAD/Design planning tasks. During JAD/Design, the user representatives are typically more of a mixed group. Because they will be providing the design details, their composition must reflect the scope of the system, and may include managers of every level, staff assistants, professionals, and clerical employees from one or more departments of the organization.

The user representatives participate full time during the JAD session phases to which they have been assigned and participate sporadically during the corresponding customization and wrap-up phases. During customization, the user representatives prepare their thoughts and gather any reference material they deem appropriate for the JAD session to come. During the session phase, the session leader guides the user representatives and other participants through the JAD tasks to define requirements and/or develop a design. During wrap-up, the user representatives review the completed JAD document and, in the case of JAD/Design, review the prototype as well. They also present the JAD/Design results to the executive sponsor.

The ideal user representative has considerable experience on the job and knowledge of the organizational environment. He or she should be a creative, innovative thinker, a good listener, and unafraid to speak up in a group situation. A user representative who lacks either knowledge of other departments pertinent to the design, knowledge of computer systems, or knowledge of JAD will be briefed in all of these areas during the course of the JAD. However, a user representative with a background in these areas is certainly a plus. User representatives should be positive, upbeat team players who are willing to work hard with others in order to make a significant contribution.

INFORMATION SYSTEMS REPRESENTATIVE

The information systems representative provides guidance and advice within the JAD context. He or she makes suggestions and provides information about the users' opportunities and trade-offs. The role of the information systems representative is threefold: help users to take advantage of the information systems resource, help to steer users away from designing a "blue sky" system that is not implementable, and learn the users' perspective.

Many times user representatives, unfamiliar with all that the information systems resource can do for them, will limit their design solutions to the little that they have seen of the computer world. For example, a user accustomed to a batch punch card accounting system would be unlikely to design a system that takes advantage of existing online technology, personal computer to mainframe accessibility, or spreadsheet analysis software tools. The user may create a system that duplicates data entry work effort because he or she does not consider interfaces to other existing systems within the organization. Thus it is the information systems representative's responsibility to advise the user representatives of their options within the course of the JAD discussions.

Simultaneously, the information systems representatives must advise the user representatives of any trade-offs. Their purpose is to provide information rather than to grant or deny the users permission. If the user representatives are discussing solutions that are convoluted, impractical, or not cost-effective from a technical standpoint, the information systems representatives should explain these facts and suggest alternatives. They should inform the user representatives if they are relying on risky, untested technology or if they are deviating from the organization's information systems strategy.

The information systems representatives should learn the system design so that they can "hit the ground running" for the follow-on phases of the project. The information systems representatives for the JAD/Designs typically play key roles in the subsequent technical effort. During the course of the JADs they learn the requirements and/or external design of the system and can begin to think about its technical implementation. It is important to note that this is purely a thought process; no discussion of the technical implementation occurs within the context of the JAD sessions.

A typical JAD will have one or two information systems representatives assigned to it. They participate sporadically during the JAD customization phase, full time during the session phase, and either full time or sporadically during wrap-up. During customization, the information systems representatives typically gather materials that they may need for the session (e.g., data dictionary listings for potentially interfacing existing systems). During the session phase they listen to the user representatives' discussion and offer their advice and ideas as well. During wrap-up for JAD/Design, they may work full time on the prototype. They participate in the review process and may also assist the users with the executive sponsor presentation.

An information systems representative should have a technical background and a firm grasp on the organization's information system's strategy and capabilities. He or she should be a good communicator and be able to deal effectively with other people. Typically, information systems representatives are either key players in the follow-on technical effort, such as the architect, database designer, manager, or technical leader, or they represent a tightly coupled interfacing system. If the information system representative is to develop a system prototype, he or she should also be proficient in the prototyping software. During the JAD/Plan session, information systems executives may also participate.

SPECIALIST

The role of the specialist is to provide expertise on a defined, limited topic. He or she is the only part-time participant in the session. Specialists may have a user or information systems background and attend only those sessions that pertain directly to their area of expertise.

An example of a user area specialist would be the individual whose sole use of the system is limited to a single report or inquiry screen. He or she would participate in the session on the day that the particular function was being designed. Information systems specialists are frequently individuals with expertise in other interfacing systems within the organization. The extent to which they participate would vary according to the criticality and impact of the interface.

During customization, the specialist may gather materials in a similar fashion as the user representative or information systems representative. During the session phase, the specialist is scheduled to participate for a limited amount of time. Prior to their participation, specialists are briefed as to what decisions have been made during the session to date. This briefing is usually done by the session leader and one or two other participants. During wrap-up, the specialist participates in the review process and attends the executive sponsor presentation.

The specialist obviously must have a solid background in the area in which he or she is being asked to provide expertise. The specialist should be able to grasp quickly what has already been decided during earlier group sessions and understand how his or her part of the design will fit into the overall scheme. In addition, the specialist should have good interpersonal skills.

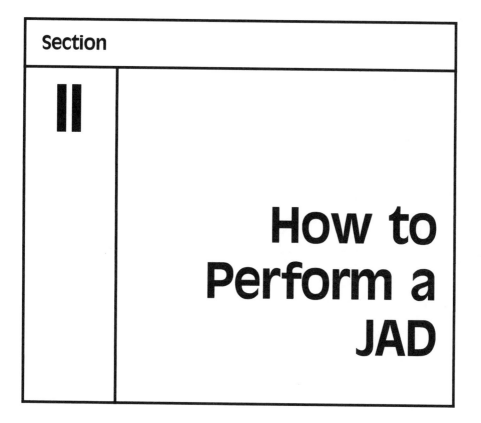

Section

II

How to Perform a JAD

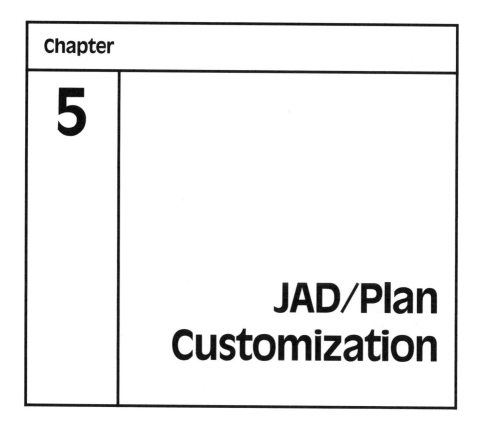

Chapter

5

JAD/Plan Customization

JAD/Plan customization is the first phase of a JAD development project. At the outset of this phase, individuals within the organization have come up with an idea for a system. They have generated enough support for the project for funds to have been allocated and staff committed for the JAD/Plan activity.

The purpose of the JAD/Plan customization phase is to prepare for the subsequent JAD/Plan session phase, during which the system's high-level requirements and scope will be determined. If the customization tasks are accomplished effectively, a more rewarding session and a minimum of participants' time will result. Since the JAD/Plan session phase involves the participation of executives, managers, and other key employees, a productive, professionally run session is well worth the customization effort.

The customization phase for the JAD/Plan typically lasts from one to five days, depending primarily on the size and complexity of the project. The organization's JAD experience and resources, as well as the depth of experience of the session leader and analysts, will also affect the length of the customization phase.

The session leader and one or two analysts are the primary participants in the customization phase for the JAD/Plan. In preparing for the session phase, they may meet with one or more of the other designated JAD/Plan session participants on an as-needed basis. In addition, all session participants spend some time jotting down their ideas for the system, so they will be prepared for the discussions to take place in session.

The major tasks performed during the JAD/Plan customization phase are the following:

- Conduct orientation.
- Organize JAD/Plan team.
- Tailor tasks and outputs.
- Prepare materials for session.

CONDUCT ORIENTATION

The session leader and analysts assigned to the project must gain an understanding of the project to date. This is not an in-depth study of the current manual or automated system but, rather, a broad overview. The session leader and analysts must resist the temptation to revert to more traditional methods in which they would attempt to learn the business and then design the system themselves. Instead, they should confine their effort to gaining an appreciation of the project status, as well as obtaining a general background of the organization, the nature and operations of its business, and any special terminology in use.

Often the JAD session leader and analysts begin their effort on the project after some preliminary work has already been completed. For example, the users may have had a number of meetings to discuss their ideas for the system before the decision was made to proceed with the JAD/Plan. Commitments may have been made during these meetings that have an impact on project viability and success. Potential project snags and issues may have already surfaced. The session leader and analysts may gain insight into the project by reading meeting summary memos that may have been generated. Briefings by other players who were present may provide additional background.

The session leader and analysts may also require some background on the nature and operations of the organization and the people to be involved in the project. Often the session leader and analysts will come from a "consulting" group, either internal or external to the organization. They will need to learn which departments will be affected by the system, their functions, the key individuals in those departments, and any specialized terminology. This information will help the session leader and analysts to follow the discussions better during the session phases of the JAD/Plan and JAD/Design(s). It will also help the session leader to know to whom questions and issues should be addressed, as well as to understand some of the motivations and sensitivities underlying the group dynamics of the sessions.

Familiarization with the organization and its people may be accomplished in part by looking at an organization chart. The session leader and analysts may also want to discuss with some of the key users how each department and the people in it relate to the system objective in order to gain an overview of the business and terminology. In this context, participants will often warn the session leader and analysts about the character and personality of other participants. This type of briefing should always be taken with a grain of salt; it occasionally reflects more about the informant than the person being discussed.

ORGANIZE JAD/PLAN TEAM

The session leader and executive sponsor are responsible for organizing the participants for the JAD/Plan session. They ensure that all of the appropriate individuals are advised that they are JAD/Plan participants. The goal is to avoid being in the middle of the session phase and discover that a required person is not present. In addition, the session leader should explain to the participants what is expected of them so that they can be better prepared for the session.

Select or Confirm Participants

Depending on when the session leader is brought onto the project, the participants for the JAD/Plan may or may not have already been selected. Even if a participant list has already been developed, the session leader should make sure that no one was overlooked. Having become familiar with the departments and key players involved in the system during the orientation tasks, the session leader is in a position to help determine that all necessary skills and inputs are represented among the participants. The executive sponsor is often the most able to determine whether or not an individual should be included at the JAD/Plan stage of the project. At a minimum, the executive sponsor should confirm the decision to include an individual before that person is requested to attend.

In the case of the Sales Processing and Reporting (SUPER) system, the JAD/Plan participants are selected from the higher levels of the organization, and include the vice president of sales (who is the executive sponsor), a regional manager, a branch manager, a key headquarters marketing analyst, the information systems architect and database designer, two JAD analysts, and a session leader. Figure 5-1 shows where the user participants are positioned on an organization chart.

Prepare Participants

The session leader must inform each participant of the dates, times, and place of the JAD/Plan session. In addition, the session leader should explain the objectives and agenda for the session phase and should review how the participants might prepare for the session discussions. Participant preparation varies, depending on whether the participant is from a user department, information systems group, or is a JAD analyst.

The users are asked to jot down notes on problems they are experiencing in current operations, as well as their view of the high-level requirements (objectives,

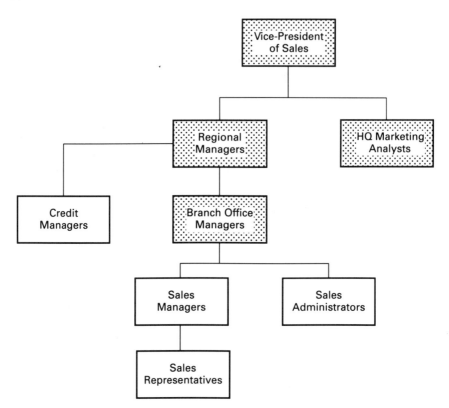

Figure 5-1 User area organization chart for SUPER system, highlighting the JAD/Plan participants.

anticipated benefits, strategic and future considerations, constraints, assumptions, audit and control requirements) and the system scope. The session leader can provide the users with examples and thought-provoking questions to aid their thought process. The users are also asked to bring with them any reference material that might be helpful, such as currently used forms. For example, the SUPER system JAD/Plan user representatives might bring manual order forms they currently use to help determine approximately how much data must be entered on an order. This will be of assistance during the estimating task to be performed during the JAD/Plan session.

Information systems representatives should begin to consider what the system's hardware and/or software constraints and assumptions might be. In addition, the information systems representatives should investigate the status of potential interfacing systems to determine whether any rewrites or major modifications are planned. Some of these enhancements may influence the decisions made during the JAD/Plan session.

Ideally, the analyst will have had prior JAD experience. Frequently, though, the analyst is a programmer who has never participated in a JAD. Analysts must be trained in the methodology before the session begins. They must understand the JAD tasks and be completely familiar with the output formats. Once trained in the methodology, the analyst must coordinate with the session leader to determine the logistics of the documentation effort during the session phase. If there are two analysts, will they alternate taking notes and entering data into the documentation system? Will there be a documentation system in the session room? Which of the session results will the session leader record on transparencies or flip charts, eliminating the need for an analyst to take notes on them? The session leader and analyst should run through each of the session tasks and determine how each will be recorded.

TAILOR TASKS AND OUTPUTS

During the JAD/Plan customization phase, the JAD tasks and outputs are reviewed and tailored. The goal is to adjust the tasks, JAD/Plan and JAD/Design documents, and prototype in order to make them as appropriate as possible for both the organization and the specific nature of the project. During JAD/Plan customization, the tasks and outputs for both JAD/Plan and JAD/Design are examined. This is because the session leader must be able to estimate the length of the JAD/Design(s) during the JAD/Plan session phase; changes to the JAD/Design process or outputs may affect those estimates.

In order to tailor JAD for the organization, the session leader reviews the standard JAD formats and contents with the information systems department manager as well as a quality assurance representative, if appropriate. If the organization uses a documentation software package that imposes specific standards, an expert on the software should also participate in the meeting. This organizational level tailoring should occur the first time the organization performs a JAD and at any future time when the organization implements a major change in the standards, such as the purchase and use of a new documentation software package.

When deciding how to tailor the JAD process and outputs, the session leader must adhere to the four major JAD tenets (see Chap. 1):

- Facilitated group session approach
- Effective use of visual aids to illustrate objectives, requirements, and design
- Organized, rational process
- What you see is what you get documentation approach

The results of the meeting to tailor the process and outputs should be clearly documented and may be incorporated into the organization's information systems standards and guidelines. This will enable all participants on the current project as well as participants on subsequent JAD projects to readily access and understand the new standards.

Regardless of whether JAD was previously tailored to the organization, the session leader should review the process and outputs in light of the idiosyncrasies of the specific project. For example, the most experienced marketing analyst may be transferring to another division just prior to the SUPER system JAD/Plan session. Although another qualified marketing analyst will participate in the session, the session leader may arrange to meet with the transferring analyst during JAD/Plan customization. The marketing analyst could provide preliminary answers in the form of bullet items for the requirements and scope topics. All of the other participants would subsequently review and refine the marketing analyst's ideas during the JAD/Plan session.

PREPARE MATERIALS FOR SESSION

The session leader and analyst work together to prepare the necessary materials for the session phase. They focus on three areas:

- Arranging for the session room, equipment, and materials
- Preparing visual aids
- Setting up the session room

Arrange for the Session Room, Equipment, and Materials

The session leader or the analyst coordinates with the appropriate individuals to arrange for the session room, equipment, and materials. In doing so, the first decision that must be made is whether or not to hold the session off-site, such as in another organization-owned facility or in a local hotel. The major advantage to holding the session at a site other than the participants' primary work location is that the participants are less likely to be interrupted or distracted by the continuing demands of their jobs. In any case, a conference room must be booked in advance of the session dates.

Session support equipment, such as an overhead projector, flip chart stands, and magnetic board, must also be scheduled. In addition, markers, flip chart paper, a spare overhead projector bulb, transparencies, and paper and pencils must be ordered. The reusable vinyl JAD data element and process block magnetics must either be ordered or, if the organization already has the magnetics, scheduled and cleaned.[1] Depending on when the session will be held, appropriate meals and/or refreshments may be requested.

Prepare Visual Aids

The session leader and analyst must prepare the visual aids for the JAD/Plan session. Figure 5-2 lists typical visual aids. Whether to use flip charts or transparen-

---

[1]The magnetics are washable vinyl rectangles with magnetic strips on the back. The data element magnetics measure 1.5 inches by 7.5 inches. The process block magnetics measure 5.0 inches by 7.5 inches. See Appendix E for ordering information.

    ✔ JAD Introductory Presentations

    ✔ Requirements Topics
        Objectives
        Anticipated benefits
        Strategic and future considerations
        Constraints and assumptions
        Security, audit, and control

    ✔ Scope Topics
        System users
        System locations
        In-scope (functional areas)
        Out-of-scope (functional areas)

    ✔ Estimating Assumptions Forms

    ✔ Participant List/Matrix Form

    ✔ JAD Identification Forms

    ✔ Issues Forms

    ✔ Considerations

    ✔ Session Agenda

    ✔ "Welcome" Flip Chart (with system name).

Figure 5-2   List of JAD/Plan visual aids.

cies for these visual aids depends on a number of factors, including the amount of wall space in the session room and the availability of an overhead projector. A flip chart hung on a wall has the advantage of constantly being on display; this is particularly useful for the more important items such as the requirements and scope. On the other hand, it is convenient to photocopy standard formats and prepared write-ups onto transparencies. They are also easier to transport and are somewhat (messily) erasable.

JAD introductory presentation.   The session leader should prepare a presentation to introduce the participants to the JAD methodology. This introduction may be based on a generic JAD presentation that the session leader developed previously but should be modified to incorporate any tailoring of the JAD tasks and outputs (refer to the tailoring task of JAD/Plan customization). The presentation should provide the participants with an overview of the entire JAD methodology, as well as a more detailed understanding of JAD/Plan. Samples of JAD/Plan outputs help the participants to grasp what is expected of them.

Requirements and scope.   Flips or transparencies are prepared for the high-level requirements and system scope (see Fig. 5-3). Each topic has a separate

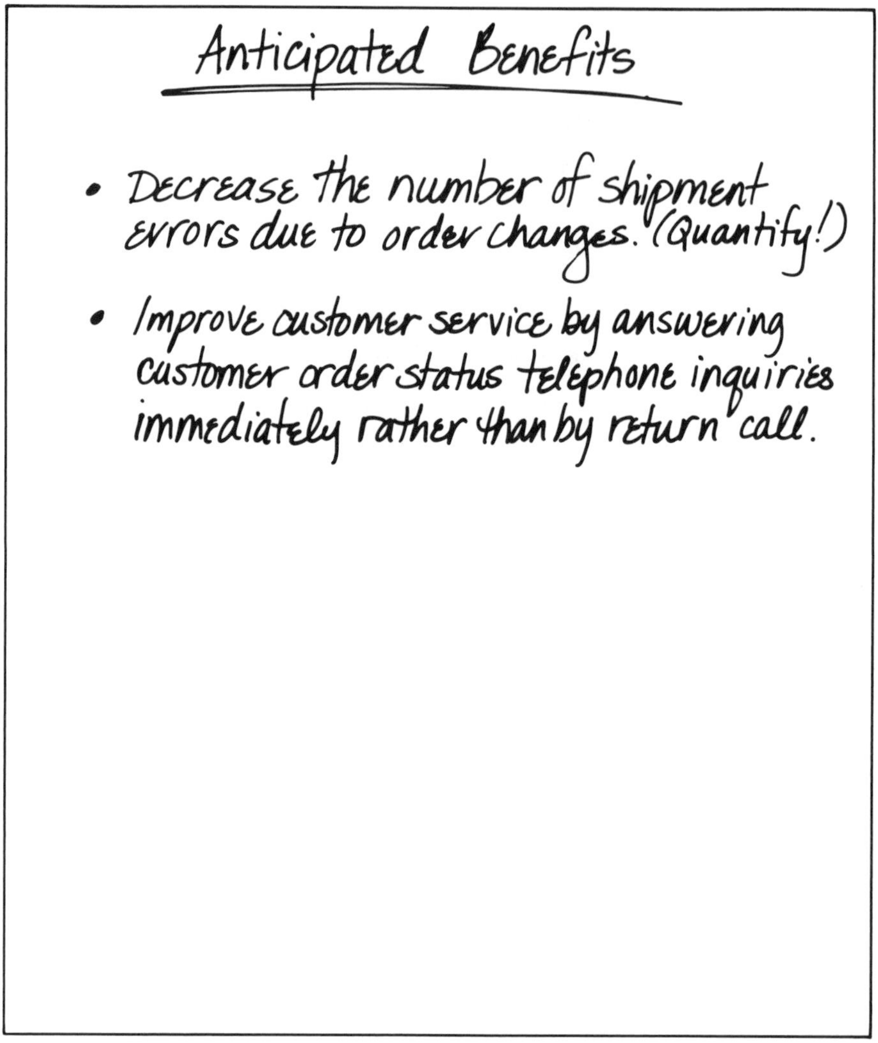

Anticipated Benefits

- Decrease the number of shipment errors due to order changes. (Quantify!)

- Improve customer service by answering customer order status telephone inquiries immediately rather than by return call.

Figure 5-3   Sample requirements flip chart. The session leader has extracted bulleted items from project memos.

flip chart or transparency. The session leader and analyst place a heading at the top of the flip or transparency. They then fill in preliminary answers based on information obtained during the orientation task. The answers are phrased as bullet-item text rather than as paragraphs. Some topics may have multiple bullet items, and other topics may have none. These bullet items will be refined and expanded upon in session.

Estimating assumptions, participant list/matrix, and JAD/Design identification forms.   Figures 5-4, 5-5, and 5-6 illustrate the blank formats for

ESTIMATING ASSUMPTIONS

JAD/Design Name:

JAD/Design Abbreviation:

Phase   **Estimates**

Customization

Session

Wrap-up

Estimating Inputs:

Figure 5-4   Estimating assumptions form.

the estimating assumptions, participant list/matrix, and JAD/Design identification forms. All three are used during the JAD/Plan session phase to plan the JAD/Design (see Chap. 6). Transparencies are an effective visual aid for these forms. A master hard copy of each form may be copied onto multiple transparencies for use during the session. The number of transparency copies needed will depend on the anticipated size of the system; one estimating assumptions form plus one JAD/Design

PARTICIPANT MATRIX FORM

Participant Name	Super System JAD/Design	

Legend: JAD Roles
E = Executive sponsor
U = User representative
I = Information systems representative
S = Specialist
A = Analyst
J = JAD session leader

Figure 5-5   Participant matrix form.

identification form is needed for each JAD/Design planned. The participant list/ matrix must have room in which to write all of the participants' names. It never hurts to make extra copies of each form.

Issues and considerations.   The session leader and analyst prepare issues and considerations flip charts or transparencies. In JAD, an issue is a

JAD/DESIGN IDENTIFICATION

JAD/Design Name:

JAD/Design Abbreviation:

Phase   **Dates**   **Exceptions/Notes**

Customization

Session

Wrap-up

Procedures

Figure 5-6   JAD/Design identification form.

discussion item that affects the scope covered in session but cannot be resolved directly by the participants. The participants either lack the authority or information to resolve the item and must go outside the session for resolution. A consideration is an item outside the scope covered in session. It may affect the business in general, a subsequent release of the system, another system, or another JAD scope.

The issues visual aid is formatted in columns, with blank areas to be filled in with the date the issue arose, a brief description, the participant to whom the issue is assigned for follow-up, and a resolution date and description (see Fig. 5-7). The considerations visual usually contains a heading and is left blank for bullet-item text to be added during the session.

Agenda and welcome.   The agenda flip chart may span one or more pages. During the session phase, the agenda flip chart helps the session leader and

ISSUES				
Issue Date	Issue Description	Assign To	Resolution Date	Resolution Description

Figure 5-7 Issues form.

participants to remember which task and topic is to be addressed next (I often refer to it as my "cheat sheet"). At a minimum, the agenda lists the session tasks in bullet format (e.g., define high-level requirements, bound system scope). It may also contain specific topics (e.g., the list of requirements and scope topics to be covered), as well as any other reminders the session leader considers helpful.

The welcome flip chart adds to the professional look of the session room and ensures that the participants see the system name or acronym in writing. The SUPER system JAD/Plan flip chart would read "Welcome to the SUPER system JAD/Plan." Small drawings or decorations can add some flair to the flip and may reflect the subject matter of the JAD or the time of year (e.g., pumpkins for Halloween).

Set Up the Session Room

Setting up the session room is usually done the afternoon prior to the session phase. The session leader and analysts arrange the seating, hang the flip charts, and set up the overhead projector, magnetic board, and the automated documentation system, if used.

The visual aids should be placed so that they are easily viewed given the seating arrangement chosen. When hanging flip charts on the walls, it is advisable to place blank sheets of paper behind them. Some of the markers bleed through standard flip chart paper—better to have a duplicate set of the requirements on the backup flip chart papers than on the conference room walls. Whenever possible, a nonglare surface should be planned for projecting the transparencies. Effectively placed visual aids provide participants with readily accessible reference points and mind joggers during the session phase.

The session leader and analysts determine the seating arrangement based on room size and number of participants. Since JAD/Plan sessions are usually in small to medium-sized conference rooms and with an average of five participants, seating is often around a conference table. A horseshoe arrangement is an alternative frequently used for larger sessions. A good seating arrangement will promote open discussions among all participants.

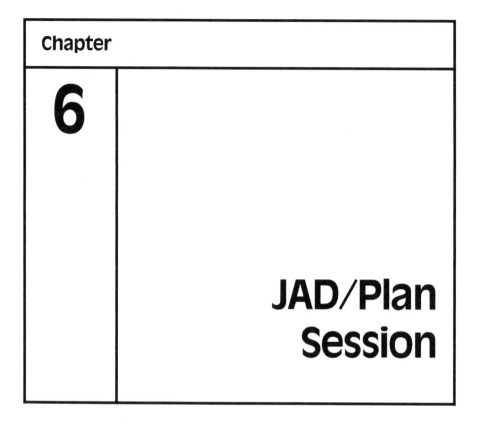

Chapter

6

JAD/Plan Session

The JAD/Plan session phase sets up the system target and plans the JAD/Design activities needed to hit a bull's-eye. It accomplishes most of the work performed in the traditional objectives phase of the software development life cycle. The JAD/Plan participants meet in a group session to specify the system's high-level requirements, define the system scope, and plan the JAD/Design effort.

During the earlier phase of JAD/Plan customization, the session leader, analysts, and other participants accomplished tasks to prepare for the session. At the start of the session phase, individuals may have their own ideas about the system and may seem to have a vague notion of what the system should encompass. However, it is not until the JAD/Plan session phase that all of the necessary participants discuss and analyze the ideas together in an organized fashion. Their decisions build the foundation of the system design.

Prior to or during JAD/Plan customization, the session leader and executive sponsor decide who should participate in the JAD/Plan session. They generally look to department managers and key employees in order to staff the session with a fairly high-level, tactical perspective. For a small, contained system, the executive sponsor may be able to provide most, if not all, of the information needed. The session will then take on the flavor of a small group interview. In larger systems, the participants may include a number of user and information systems representatives as well as one or more specialists. In either case, the session leader facilitates the session and the analyst records the session results.

The JAD/Plan session phase usually lasts from one to five days, depending on the size and complexity of the system. A small system's session can be accomplished within one day, a medium-sized system requires two to three days, and a large system requires four to five days. For example, the SUPER system is a medium-sized system of average complexity. Two session days therefore will be allocated.

Over the course of the JAD/Plan session, the session leader guides the participants through eight tasks:

- Conduct orientation.
- Define high-level requirements.
- Bound system scope.
- Identify and estimate JAD/Designs.
- Identify JAD/Design participants.
- Schedule JAD/Designs.
- Document issues and considerations.
- Conclude session phase.

CONDUCT ORIENTATION

Kickoff Presentation

Orientation during the JAD/Plan session phase is aimed at expanding the participants' understanding of the project history and the JAD methodology. Much of the orientation is accomplished during an initial *kickoff* presentation. The executive sponsor usually begins by welcoming everyone to the session and provides a short project history. He or she gives the participants an appreciation for the importance of the project, what events have occurred to date, and the expectations the organization has set for the group.

The session leader then presents an introduction to the JAD methodology. He or she provides overview information on the following topics:

- ✔ What is JAD?
- ✔ Participant roles
- ✔ JAD structure (activities, phases)
- ✔ JAD outputs
- ✔ Session times and rules
- ✔ Benefits of JAD

At this point the session leader avoids bombarding the participants with too many details. Rather, they should gain an overall flavor of what JAD involves and should have fairly accurate expectations of what JAD can produce.

Detailed Task Explanations

The details of the JAD/Plan session are presented gradually during the course of the session. The session leader provides the participants with an orientation to each new task as they are about to perform that task. This includes a task description, an explanation of what purpose the task serves, a description of how the group will accomplish the task, and how the result is to be formatted. Sample outputs enable the participants to visualize what it is they are trying to achieve.

DEFINE HIGH-LEVEL REQUIREMENTS

The session leader guides the participants through the task of identifying and agreeing on the needs that the system should fulfill. The participants address five major topics:

- **Objectives.** What are the objectives of this project? Why are we developing this system? What purpose should it serve?
- **Anticipated benefits.** What benefits do we expect to derive from this system? Can these benefits be quantified (e.g., cost savings, increased revenues, efficiency, decision support)? What are the intangible benefits (e.g., job satisfaction, morale)?
- **Strategic and future considerations.** Can this system provide us with strategic advantages? What changes can be foreseen in the future operating environment of the organization (e.g., changes in the customer base, suppliers, competitors, government, or legal environment or changes within our own organization)? How can the system enable us to be more effective, efficient, and competitive in the future?
- **Constraints and assumptions.** Are there any constraints or assumptions for the system or the development project? Do any financial or time limitations exist? Are there any organizational or personnel constraints or assumptions? Are there specific hardware, software, or interface assumptions?
- **Security, audit and control.** What are the broad security requirements for the system? Are there audit and control points that must be considered?

In defining high-level requirements, the participants are forced to step back from the current way of operating and reexamine what the system should do for them. This helps to avoid the frequently encountered downfall of designing a system that is merely a variation on the current environment. By critically evaluating the system target, the participants broaden their perspective and let their initiative and creativity take over.

The session leader asks the participants to address each of the five topics individually. He or she identifies the current topic, reviews any existing responses for that topic,[1] and encourages the participants to voice their ideas. As ideas are generated, the session leader or analyst documents them in bullet format on either the flip charts or transparencies prepared during JAD/Plan customization. The participants then evaluate and refine the bullet items.

As an example, the SUPER system session leader prepares a flip chart for each of the five topics. On the flip chart for assumptions and constraints, the session leader extracts the following bullet item from a memo reviewed during JAD/Plan customization:

- System users will have access to a user-friendly ad hoc reporting facility.

The participants review and refine this bullet item and then generate additional points themselves. For example, they may add such bullet items as

- The system must be flexible enough to expeditiously handle changes to the sales force and product line.
- Although all sales representatives will eventually have access to the system from the road and customer sites via laptop PCs, this may be phased in over time, as the budget allows.

When the session leader and participants are satisfied that the current topic has been fully covered, the session leader identifies the next topic for discussion. Refinements may be made at any time to previous topics.

BOUND SYSTEM SCOPE

At the outset of the JAD/Plan session phase, the participants usually agree on a general notion of what the eventual system will encompass. However, they may have different opinions about the more specific system scope areas and in fact may not have even considered some of the more innovative areas. After the high-level requirements have been identified in the session, the participants focus on defining a system scope that will address the organization's needs.

Nailing down the overall system scope up front in the design process serves two major purposes. First, it lays a foundation of agreement on which both the JAD/Plan and the JAD/Design participants can build. This is particularly helpful in a multi-JAD/Design project where the participants designing a given subsystem can see how the subsystem relates back to the whole. The second purpose is for better project management. During the course of the JADs, the session leader and participants have a way to gauge whether they are on track. They can check to ensure that the design covers the entire scope and whether the bounds of the scope

---

[1]During JAD/Plan customization, the session leader and analyst may have extracted bullet-item text from project memos or other documentation.

are being inappropriately expanded. In addition, the more specifically the scope is defined, the better the project estimates can be and the easier it is to exercise change management and control policies.

Outline the System Scope

The session leader initiates the scope definition task by asking the participants to identify the job categories or types of people who will be using the system, as well as the physical locations of individuals who will have access to the system. This is not intended to be a detailed description about specific individuals who are to have personal computers on their desks, for example. Instead, it is a more general definition that requires the participants to envision how the system is to operate logistically and functionally. The session leader documents the results in bullet format text on the flip charts or transparencies prepared during JAD/Plan customization.

In the case of the SUPER system, for example, the participants may come up with the following bullet items:

SUPER SYSTEM SCOPE

- The following groups of people are considered users of the system:
  - Sales representatives
  - Sales managers
  - Branch office managers
  - Sales administrators
  - Credit managers
  - Regional managers
  - Headquarters marketing analysts
  - Vice president of sales
- The system will be available to users in the following locations:
  - Branch offices
  - Regional offices
  - Headquarters marketing department
  - With sales force on the road and at customer sites (phased in over time)

The session leader then asks the participants to focus on what are termed *procedures*. A procedure is a fairly high-level functional piece of the system being designed. It is usually expressed as a verb and an object, such as "accept orders," "produce shipping documents," or "analyze sales achievements." Although a system can be divided into procedures by a variety of ways, it is often easiest to approach the task sequentially, coming up with a procedure and then asking, "So, what major planning step or group of activities should happen next?"[2]

---

[2]In his book *User-Centered Requirements Analysis*, Charles F. Martin identifies four alternatives to top-level decomposition of a system: by user type, by planning and productions steps, by input-processing-output, and by functional area [6].

The session leader encourages the participants to list all of the procedures that are to be included in the system scope. As the users contribute their ideas, the session leader or analyst writes each procedure on its own erasable magnetic card (the "process blocks"; see Appendix E) and places the magnetics on a magnetic board.

Within the course of the scope discussion, the session leader also encourages the participants to specify areas that are outside the system scope. These may be items that are totally outside the scope or items that are outside the scope for the current release or version of the system but may be considered for a subsequent, enhanced release. The session leader lists these out-of-scope items on the flip chart or transparency prepared during JAD/Plan customization. He or she asks the participants to distinguish which items may be included in a subsequent release.

Again, using the SUPER system as an example, the flip chart may have the following bullet items:

OUT OF SCOPE

- The following items may be available in a subsequent release of the SUPER system but are currently considered out of scope:
  - Marketing promotions processing, analysis, and reporting
  - Computer modeling of the marketing environment for a decision support system
- The following items are out of scope for the SUPER system:
  - Generating invoices
  - Calculating and processing sales force commissions

Develop Business Flow Diagram

Once the participants feel assured that they have identified most if not all of the procedures, they come up to the board and manipulate the procedure magnetics in order to create a high-level diagram, called a *business flow diagram* (see Fig. 6-1). The participants draw connecting arrows between the magnetic blocks with erasable dry markers. When new ideas arise, changes in the procedures and arrows are easily and neatly accommodated by the erasable magnetic medium. Participants usually find this a fun, creative task as they begin to mold the system into shape.

When the participants seem to agree on a final business flow diagram, the session leader asks them to review the high-level requirements and scope items in order to ensure that all of the identified needs are accommodated by the design. Final adjustments to either the requirements, scope, or the business flow diagram may need to be made.

Once finalized, the business flow diagram must be copied onto a more permanent medium. The analyst can copy the diagram onto a transparency or flip chart while the session leader introduces the participants to the next task. For legibility, it is easier to copy a larger diagram onto a transparency. However, when a transparency is used, it is helpful to list the procedures on a flip chart as well. The

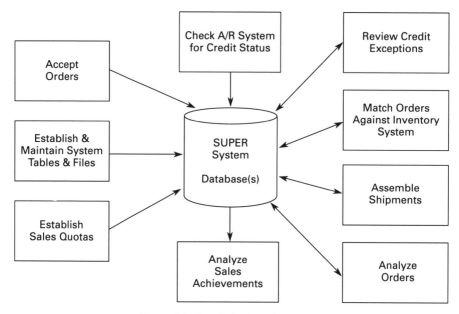

Figure 6-1   Sample business flow diagram.

in-scope items are important references for the participants and should remain in constant view.

IDENTIFY AND ESTIMATE JAD/DESIGNS

Gather Estimating Data

Once the overall system scope has been defined, the session leader gathers more detailed estimating data from the participants. The session leader has the group break down each of the procedures in order to determine the anticipated screen and report layouts, processing routines, and system interfaces. The goal of this task is to generate accurate estimates for the JAD/Design(s). Participants in the JAD/Design however, will not be constrained by this list; they may eventually make decisions that alter the items included for any given procedure.[3]

For example, the SUPER system session leader may start with the procedure "accept orders" and ask the participants how many major types of orders they have and how many pieces of data they collect about each one. The approximate number of data elements will help the session leader to determine if the order function will

---

[3]In fact, it is normal to overlook some of the functions during the JAD/Plan. Because of the higher level perspective of the JAD/Plan participants and the broader scope of the discussion, some of the functions that will eventually be thought of during the JAD/Design are not factored into the original estimates. The estimating rules of thumb tend to take some of this into account.

entail one screen layout or more. The session leader also asks the participants if the procedure involves any reports, interfaces, or major processing steps. The participants indicate that pricing of the orders is an extensive, complex processing routine. The session leader or analyst records a bullet format list of the screen layouts, reports, major processing routines, and interfaces. These bullets will eventually be documented on the estimating assumptions form (see Fig. 6-2).

ESTIMATING ASSUMPTIONS

JAD/Design Name: Order Processing and Reporting

JAD/Design Abbreviation: OP&R

Phase	Estimates
Customization	4 days
Session	6 days
Wrap-up	9 days

Estimating Inputs:

- Customer Data Screen
- Order Data Screens—3
- Product Data Screen
- Credit Review Screen
- Inquiry Screens—4
- Accounts Receivable Interface
- Inventory Interfaces—2
- Credit Review Processing Requirements
- Pricing Processing Requirements
- Backlog Report
- Sales Order Report
- Packing List Report
- Bill of Lading Report
- Management Reports—2
- Menus

Figure 6-2 Sample estimating assumptions.

For an obviously medium to large system, the session leader may ask the participants to divide the overall system into logical subsystems for JAD/Designs. In the case of the SUPER system, the participants identify a sales management JAD/Design, encompassing the two procedures "establish quotas" and "analyze sales achievements." They group the remaining procedures in a second JAD/Design called order processing and reporting.

Estimate the JAD/Design(s)

When all of the estimating data have been gathered, the session leader may call a break in the session during which time he or she can examine the estimating inputs and determine the length(s) of the JAD/Design(s).

The session leader estimates the JAD/Design session phase first. He or she begins by generating task-by-task estimates, especially if there has been significant tailoring of the standard JAD tasks and outputs. The experience level of the session leader, analysts, and other participants should be taken into account, as well as the apparent degree of complexity and potential controversy surrounding the system. The more new ground that the system will break, the more extensive the discussions will be and the longer each task will take. The task-by-task estimates for the session phase can then be compared against the estimating rules of thumb (see worksheets in Appendix A) and analyzed for any discrepancies.

For example, the SUPER system task-by-task estimates for the order processing and reporting JAD/Design came out to six session days. The session leader then completes the estimating rules of thumb worksheet (see Appendix B) and is comfortable that the estimates are confirmed. The session leader maintains the six-day session phase estimate.

The session leader then determines if the division of scope into subsystems for JAD/Design(s) is valid. This decision is based on the desire to keep the session phase for each JAD/Design within a three- to ten-day time frame. Dividing the scope into many small JAD/Designs makes the system too fragmented and difficult for the participants to design. On the other hand, few large JAD/Designs may prove too strenuous for the participants, causing fatigue and loss of concentration. The session leader tries to find a middle ground for session phase length by adjusting the scope of the JAD/Designs. In doing so, the session leader must also be careful to keep together logically related functional units of the system.

Once the JAD/Design session phase estimates are complete and the individual JAD/Design(s) are defined, the session leader develops the estimates for customization and wrap-up. As in estimating the session phase, the session leader begins with task-by-task estimates and then confirms the results by comparing them against the estimating rules of thumb. In the case of a multi-JAD/Design system, the session leader also develops estimates for the final wrap-up.

For example, the SUPER system task-by-task estimates for the order processing and reporting customization phase came out to four days. This is less than the five and a half days from the estimating rules of thumb (see Appendix B). The session leader feels comfortable with the lower, task-by-task number because some of the more time-consuming, standard JAD/Design customization tasks will be unnecessary in this case. All of the documentation forms are already online, there is little tailoring to be done, and the session leader has JAD introductory presentations that were originally created for a previous JAD project.

The task-by-task estimates for the SUPER system order processing and reporting wrap-up phase came out to eight calendar days. The session leader then completes the estimating rules of thumb worksheet (Appendix B). The nine-and-a-half-day estimate obtained from the worksheet is close to the task-by-task number. The session leader decides to go with nine days.

Format the Estimates

The session leader and analysts prepare flip charts or transparencies listing each JAD/Design name with its estimates and the associated assumptions underneath. Figure 6-2 shows the estimating assumptions transparency prepared for one of the SUPER system JAD/Designs. With all of the estimates in hand, the session leader and the other JAD/Plan participants meet back in session. The session leader reviews the estimates with the participants, highlighting any changes that were made to the JAD/Design scopes. The participants may have some additional input, and final adjustments may be made.

IDENTIFY JAD/DESIGN PARTICIPANTS

Once the JAD/Plan participants have agreed on the JAD/Design(s) and the estimates, they identify the most qualified people to participate in each of the JAD/Designs. They must select the user representatives, information systems representatives, and any specialists needed. The JAD/Plan session leader, analysts, and executive sponsor usually remain in their roles throughout the entire JAD process (see Chap. 4 for a more detailed explanation of each of these roles). In order for the session leader to facilitate the JAD/Design sessions effectively, no more than 15 participants should be selected for any one session.

User representatives should be chosen in order to include the entire knowledge base required for the JAD/Design scope. When developing a multi-JAD/Design system, it is also advisable to include user representatives from other, tightly coupled JAD/Designs. This will help to ensure continuity and a smooth flow in the design of the overall system.

The information systems representatives are usually the same for all of the JAD/Designs in the system. They help to provide continuity to the system design while at the same time they are also learning about the system in preparation for the follow-on technical phases. The SUPER system information systems representatives will be the intended architect and database designer for the system.

Specialists are chosen to provide expertise on well-defined, contained subjects. Rather than these people sitting through an entire session unnecessarily, their time is scheduled to coincide with when their expertise will be needed. In the case of the SUPER system, the credit manager will be one of the specialists for the order processing and reporting JAD/Design. Her participation will be limited to the discussions of automatic credit review processing requirements and the design of exception credit review screen(s).

The session leader helps the JAD/Plan participants to identify the individuals for a JAD/Design by reviewing the scope flip charts, business flow diagram, and the JAD/Design estimating assumptions flip charts or transparencies. These visual aids contain the types of users, locations, and JAD/Design functionality. They serve as mind joggers to ensure that all required expertise and knowledge is fully represented in the participants. As the JAD/Plan participants identify individuals for a given JAD/Design, the session leader or analyst records them on a preformatted flip chart or transparency.

In the case of a project with one JAD/Design, the JAD/Design participants' names and JAD roles become a participant list (see Fig. 6-3). However, the list format is not effective for multi-JAD/Design projects. Participants assigned to more than one JAD/Design have a tendency to see their name listed for the first JAD/Design and look no further, not realizing that they may have multiple JAD/Design commitments. This may cause scheduling and attendance difficulties for the JAD/Design sessions. When a project has more than one JAD/Design, the participants' names and roles are recorded on a participant matrix (see Fig. 6-4). The matrix format makes it easy for any given participant to scan across the row and determine his or her JAD/Design assignment(s). Each column designates all of the participants for a given JAD/Design.

SCHEDULE JAD/DESIGNS

The task of scheduling the JAD/Design(s) consists of sequencing the JAD/Designs in a multi-JAD/Design system, deciding whether the session and wrap-up phases should be interspersed and assigning dates to each phase of the JAD/Designs.

Sequence the JAD/Designs

For a multi-JAD/Design system, the participants must decide in what order the JAD/Designs should be performed. Usually the more input-oriented JAD/Designs, termed *feeder* JADs, are sequenced before the more output-oriented, or *receiver*, JADs. Any JAD/Designs that are dependent on other JAD/Designs should be scheduled after the other JAD/Designs so as to benefit from the decisions made and knowledge gained. All else being equal, it is helpful to schedule a smaller, less complex JAD/Design earlier in the process to help build project momentum.

Decide on a Phase Strategy

Once the participants have agreed on the sequence for the JAD/Designs, they decide on a strategy for performing the phases. There are three major alternatives for the participants to consider.

S.M.A.L.L. System Participant List:

Participant Name	JAD Role
Alex Ecutive	Executive sponsor
Blanche Manager	User representative
Marc Keting	User representative
Salley Repp	User representative
Archi Teckt	Information systems representative
Zach Counting	Specialist
Ana List	Analyst
Judy Jad	Session leader

Figure 6-3 Sample participant list

Sequential phases.   The first and most obvious alternative is to perform the phases sequentially (see Fig. 6-5(a)). This is often the most appropriate choice when the JAD/Design participants are from out of town and want to complete the session phase in a short, intensive time frame.

Interspersed phases.   A second very popular alternative is to intersperse the session and wrap-up phases (see Fig. 6-5(b)). This alternative has the same

PARTICIPANT MATRIX FORM

Participant Name	Super System JAD/Design	
	OP&R	SM
Zach Counting	U	
Jane Credit	S	
Debbie Dezyner	I	I
Alex Ecutive	E	E, U
Judy Jad	J	J
Ana List	A	A
Blanche Manager	U	U
Addie Minn	U	
Reggie Nelrep		U
Marc Keting	U	
Alex Pert		S
Salley Repp	U	U
Archi Teckt	I	I
Doc Yument	A	A

Legend: JAD Roles
E = Executive sponsor
U = User representative
I = Information systems representative
S = Specialist
A = Analyst
J = JAD session leader

Figure 6-4 Sample participant matrix.

number of session and wrap-up days as the first alternative. However, they are interleaved, making each phase less intensive. The interleaving may be accomplished in several ways. For example, mornings may be devoted to the session phase and afternoons left for wrap-up. Another option is to have the session phase take place for three full days a week and the remaining two days spent performing wrap-up tasks. Any remaining wrap-up days would then be scheduled in an intensive, sequential fashion once the appropriate number of session days have been completed.

SCHEDULING STRATEGIES

Assuming a project with five customization days, five session days, and nine wrap-up days, an organization may select one of three major scheduling strategies:

M o n	T u e	W e d	T h u	F r i		M o n	T u e	W e d	T h u	F r i		M o n	T u e	W e d	T h u	F r i		M o n	T u e	W e d	T h u	F r i
C	C	C	C	C		S	S	S	S	S		W	W	W	W			W	W	W	W

(a) Sequential phases

M o n	T u e	W e d	T h u	F r i		M o n	T u e	W e d	T h u	F r i		M o n	T u e	W e d	T h u	F r i		M o n	T u e	W e d	T h u	F r i
C	C	C	C	C		S	S	S	W	W		S	S	W	W	W			W	W	W	W

(b) Interspersed phases

M o n	T u e	W e d	T h u	F r i		M o n	T u e	W e d	T h u	F r i		M o n	T u e	W e d	T h u	F r i		M o n	T u e	W e d	T h u	F r i
C	C	C	C	C		S	S	S	W	W		S	S	W	W	W			W	W	W	
						(W	W	W)				(W	W)								

(c) Overlapped. interspersed phases

Note that in the case of (c), the overlapped wrap-up days are discounted from five person-days to two and one-half person-days since the analyst will not be fully productive during the session. The two-and-one-half-person-day savings equates to one calendar wrap-up day with two full-time and one half-time people documenting.

Figure 6-5 Scheduling strategies.

Interspersing the session and wrap-up phases enables the JAD/Design user-participants to attend to the most urgent needs of their jobs during the allotted wrap-up time while still participating in the entire session phase. Although the JAD takes no more total calendar time to complete than in the first alternative, the interspersed session alternative is less intensive and tiring for the participants. In addition, the analysts, information systems representatives, and session leader can make considerable headway on the documentation and prototype efforts during the wrap-up time. Participants can review completed pieces of these outputs as the JAD/Design session progresses.

Overlapping phases.   A third alternative, which may be combined with either of the first two alternatives, is the option of overlapping phases (see Fig. 6-5(c)). For example, if there is a documentation system in the session room, one of the two analysts may be working on wrap-up tasks while the session phase is in progress. The analyst will not be as productive working in the session room as he or she would be working in isolation because he or she will want to listen with half an ear to the discussion. However, this strategy shortens the overall calendar time frame for the JAD/Design.

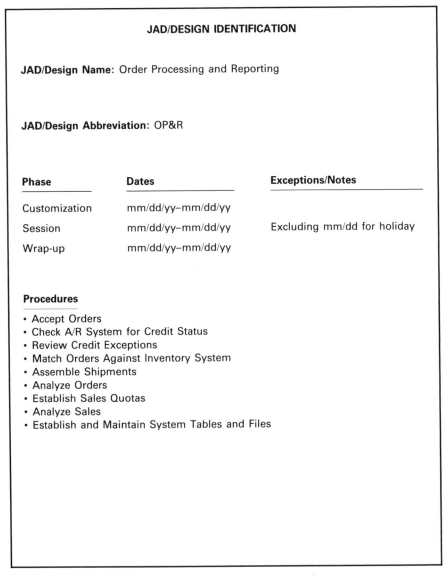

Figure 6-6 Sample JAD/design identification.

Assign Phase Dates

Once the JAD/Design sequence and the strategy for performing the phases have been agreed upon, dates are assigned to the beginning and end of each JAD/ Design phase. In scheduling the phases, care must be taken to account for holidays, year-end closings, and other potentially disruptive events. The session leader or analyst documents the JAD/Design phases and their corresponding dates on the JAD/Design identification form (see Fig. 6-6). Notes regarding holidays and other

ISSUES				
Issue Date	Issue Description	Assign To	Resolution Date	Resolution Description
1/25	Can sales management subsystem interface with commission system?	Archi Teckt	1/25	Commission system planning major rewrite. Save interface for subsequent release.
1/25	Should sales force receive commissions based purely on achievements versus quota, or should management continue to use judgment?	Alex Ecutive	1/26	Commissions to be based on achievements versus quota. Salary and promotions to incorporate judgment factors.
		. . .		

Figure 6-7 Sample issues.

exceptions are placed in the "exceptions" column. If half-day sessions are planned, then the times are specified as well. The business flow diagram procedures that apply to the given JAD/Design are specified at the bottom of the form.

DOCUMENT ISSUES AND CONSIDERATIONS

Within the course of the JAD/Plan session phase, issues and considerations may arise. An *issue* is an item that affects the JAD scope but for which the participants lack authority or information to make a decision. When an issue arises, it is assigned to a session participant for follow-up. The participant is usually someone involved in the area most affected by the issue. The session leader or analyst records the date the issue arose, a description of the issue and the person responsible for following it up (see Fig. 6-7).

The session leader begins each session day by reviewing the unresolved issues and asking the responsible participants for the resolutions. Resolutions are usually expected within 24 hours. In the case of a "show stopper" or particularly urgent issue, the resolution is sought immediately or during the next session break. The resolutions are then dated and documented on the same flip chart or transparency.

A *consideration* is an item outside the scope of the current JAD. It may affect a subsystem covered in another JAD, a later phase in the development life cycle, another system, or the business in general. Considerations are often good, productive ideas that should not be discarded just because they do not pertain to the current JAD topic. Rather than sidetracking the current JAD, such considerations are documented in bullet format for further discussion and action at a later, more appropriate time (see Fig. 6-8).

CONSIDERATIONS

• Can a regional or branch manager assign a sum total of quotas to those below him/her that is greater than his/her own quota? (For sales management JAD/Design.)

• Formal communications to the sales force must be made regarding any changes in the way commissions are currently determined. Personnel Department must be involved.

•
•
•

Figure 6-8   Sample considerations.

CONCLUDE SESSION PHASE

The session leader concludes the session phase by reviewing the accomplishments with the participants. He or she asks the participants for feedback on the results and ensures that everyone feels comfortable with the decisions made. This review fortifies the feelings of teamwork, participant ownership, and commitment.

The session leader may distribute a questionnaire for the participants to fill out in order to obtain constructive feedback on the quality of session. This will help the organization to learn from experience with the JAD methodology.

Last, the session leader may provide the participants with positive feedback as to how well they performed as a group and how creative their ideas were. This pat on the back is usually well deserved, and helps to end the session on an upbeat note. The participants will return to their normal work locations enthusiastic about the project. They will spread the word through the organization about the value and benefits of the new system and of JAD.

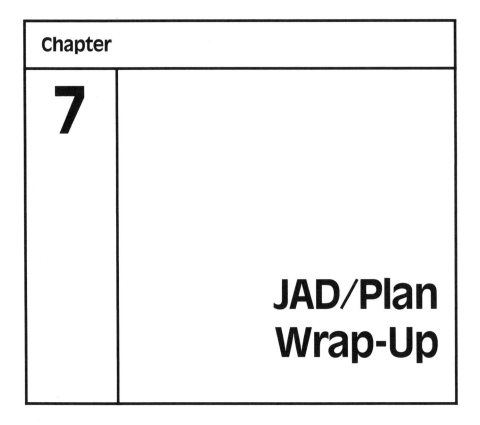

Chapter

7

JAD/Plan Wrap-Up

Form versus substance: two distinct yet intertwined elements of any subject. Substance overshadows form during the JAD/Plan session phase. The emphasis is on analysis and decision making as the session participants define the organization's requirements, establish the system scope, and plan the JAD/Design(s) to complete the effort. The JAD/Plan session decisions are recorded on visual aids and handwritten pages. During JAD/Plan wrap-up, the dominant element is form. This phase is aimed at producing, reviewing, and publishing the formal JAD/Plan document and gaining executive sponsor approval to continue with the development project.

The analysts work full time during JAD/Plan wrap-up. They have primary responsibility for transposing the outputs of the JAD/Plan session into a formal document. They are frequently assisted full time by the session leader. All of the JAD/Plan participants are asked to review the first draft of the document and to make necessary corrections. In many organizations, the information systems representative has the additional responsibility of developing project cost estimates during JAD/Plan wrap-up.[1] The executive sponsor may then compare the cost

---

[1]Although developing cost estimates is desirable at this point in the process, it is more a project management responsibility than a formal JAD task. Another project management task that should be performed throughout the course of the JAD is writing weekly status reports.

estimates with the anticipated benefits defined in the JAD/Plan document in order to make an informed decision about continued funding of the project.

The number of calendar days needed for JAD/Plan wrap-up will vary considerably, based on the system size and complexity, the amount of time allocated for participant review of the document, and the number of people working on the documentation effort. However, a fairly typical JAD/Plan wrap-up phase lasts between two and five calendar days (refer to Chap. 6 for estimating data). Following are the major tasks performed during JAD/Plan wrap-up:

- Complete the JAD/Plan document.
- Review the JAD/Plan document.
- Obtain executive sponsor approval.

COMPLETE JAD/PLAN DOCUMENT

When the JAD/Plan wrap-up phase begins, the session phase results are written on a combination of flip charts, transparencies, and paper forms. During JAD/Plan wrap-up, the analysts and session leader enter all of this material into the documentation environment. For clarity, they may find it necessary to expand on abbreviations or to embellish slightly bullet-item descriptions. However, it is not their task to rewrite completely or reformat any of the session outputs. The goal is to make the formal document as familiar to the participants as possible in order to facilitate their review of the document and maintain their feeling of ownership.

The analysts and session leader usually create a title page, table of contents, and introduction to the JAD/Plan document. Appendix C shows a sample table of contents and illustrates the order in which the JAD/Plan results are typically presented within the document. It is advisable to place the word "DRAFT" at least on the title page, if not on all of the pages of the document. This will prevent confusion in the event there are any changes as a result of the review. The introduction contains a description of the document's purpose, an overview of the JAD/Plan activity, an explanation of how to read the document (i.e., what it contains), and a brief summary of the current project status within the software development life cycle.

REVIEW JAD/PLAN DOCUMENT

All of the JAD/Plan participants are requested to review the completed JAD/Plan document. The purpose of the review is to ensure the quality of the document. It gives all participants an additional opportunity to reflect critically on their decisions and to scrutinize the resulting output.

The review task is typically approached in one of two ways. In either case the participants are asked to review the document on their own and submit to the analysts and session leader any suggested changes. In one case, a review session involving all of the participants is scheduled in advance, regardless of what changes are submitted. The session may be cancelled if there are no significant changes to discuss. In the alternative, a review session is called only if there are material changes submitted (i.e., changes more significant than corrections of typographical errors).

The analysts and session leader distribute a copy of the document to each of the JAD/Plan participants. A cover memo asks the participants to review the document, boldly mark any suggested changes either directly within the text or on a separate piece of paper, and return the updates at a given location on or before a specified date. If a review session is planned, the memo also states the date, time, and place of the review.

The suggested changes form the agenda for the review session. The session leader facilitates the discussions to analyze and make decisions about the participants' suggested changes. The analysts record the decisions and, subsequent to the review session, update the document accordingly. The "DRAFT" designation is then deleted from the document. The space may be left blank or the label "FINAL FORM" substituted.

OBTAIN EXECUTIVE SPONSOR APPROVAL

As a JAD/Plan participant, the executive sponsor had the opportunity to review the draft document and participate in the discussion of any changes. At this point, he or she is fully in agreement with the contents of the document. However, explicit executive sponsor approval in the form of a signature is a useful and important mechanism. It adds weight and authority to the document contents and officially establishes it as the system's foundation. No changes may be made to the contents of the document or the decisions described therein without the written authorization of the executive sponsor. This forms the basis of an effective change management and control policy.

The session leader or analyst usually writes a cover letter to the executive sponsor, presenting the final form of the JAD/Plan document. The letter indicates that the executive sponsor's signature in the appropriate space signifies that he or she fully accepts the contents of the JAD/Plan document as the project baseline. At the bottom of the letter there is a signature and date line for the executive sponsor's use.

The approved JAD/Plan document is then distributed to all JAD/Plan participants as well as to all of the selected JAD/Design participants. It now becomes a communications vehicle, informing all of those individuals who were not present during the JAD/Plan session about the decisions and plans made. The JAD/Plan document also serves as a reference handbook as time passes and people naturally forget exactly what was decided during the session.

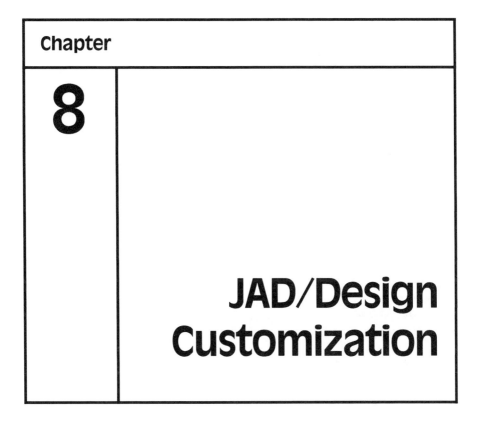

Chapter

8

JAD/Design Customization

JAD/Design customization is the first phase of the JAD/Design activity. It may follow the JAD/Plan or, in the case of a multi-JAD/Design project, it may follow an earlier JAD/Design activity. The purpose of the JAD/Design customization phase is to prepare for the JAD/Design session and wrap-up phases.

Customization for a JAD/Design typically takes from three to ten days, depending on three major factors. The first factor is the organization's JAD experience level and resources. For example, have some standard JAD presentations already been developed? Are all of the documentation formats already online? The other factors that will determine the length of JAD/Design customization are the size and complexity of the system and the experience level of the session leader and analysts assigned to the project.

The session leader and analysts perform most of the JAD/Design customization tasks. The other participants for the JAD/Design are typically involved on a limited basis during this phase. The major tasks for this phase are

- Conduct orientation.
- Organize the JAD/Design team.
- Tailor the tasks and outputs.
- Prepare materials for session.

Although these tasks are similar to those performed during JAD/Plan customization, they occur now at a more detailed level. In addition, the effort to prepare materials for the session is much more extensive during JAD/Design customization.

CONDUCT ORIENTATION

During the course of the JAD/Plan, the session leader and analysts gained an overview of the project history, organization, terminology, and the system being designed. They also worked with a few of the key users. During JAD/Design customization they expand their understanding of the specific JAD/Design subsystem.

The session leader and analysts typically begin orientation by searching for references to the particular JAD/Design in other project documentation. They review the JAD/Plan document and, in the case of a multi-JAD/Design project, previously completed JAD/Design documents as well. They pay particular attention to the requirements, issues, and considerations sections of the documents because these sections are more likely to contain material of significance to the current JAD/Design. When they find an item that applies to the JAD/Design, they incorporate that item into the session materials and agenda.

The session leader and analysts may also meet with the department manager or other key person in the JAD/Design in order to increase their understanding of the department's goals, problems, organization, and specialized terminology. This is particularly important for a multi-JAD/Design project, where the focus of the JAD/Plan is too broad to provide a full appreciation for each department or subsystem area.

As in the case of the JAD/Plan orientation task, the goal of the JAD/Design orientation is to provide the session leader and analysts with a footing or background in the area to be designed so that they can better follow and facilitate the session discussions. They try to uncover any issues or potential stumbling blocks that may affect the session. However, they leave the details and decisions regarding the requirements and design for the subsequent session phase.

ORGANIZE JAD/DESIGN TEAM

In organizing the JAD/Design team, the session leader tries to ensure that all of the selected JAD/Design participants will be present at the session and that they have adequate instructions on how to prepare themselves. To this end, the session leader confirms that the participant list is still appropriate and provides the participants with sufficient JAD and project background to enable them to prepare for the session.

Confirm Participants

In many cases the JAD/Design participants are selected during a JAD/Plan session held a few months prior to the actual performance of the JAD/Design. This situation is unavoidable for the later JAD/Designs of some multi-JAD/Design projects. However, scheduling and funding snags may cause a delay between the JAD/Plan and JAD/Design activities, even in the case of a single JAD/Design.

As time passes, changes in the organization's external environment, as well as internal factors such as organizational changes, employee transfers, and promotions, may affect the list of appropriate participants. In fact, unforeseen changes such as resignations may happen overnight. Therefore, the session leader works with the user area manager(s), information systems manager(s), and executive sponsor in order to confirm the list of participants selected during the JAD/Plan. Any changes in the list should be recorded as a change in the JAD/Plan document and approved by the executive sponsor.

Prepare Participants

After the session leader has confirmed the JAD/Design participant list, he or she informs each participant of the dates, time, and place of the JAD/Design session. In addition, the session leader explains the objectives and agenda for the session phase and reviews how the participants should prepare for the group discussions.

The session leader usually communicates all of this information via a participant preparation package that he or she puts together and distributes to the participants. In addition to informing the participants about the session logistics, the package introduces them to the JAD methodology, instructs them on how to prepare for the session phase, and sets their expectations as to what they will produce.

The JAD introductory material and output descriptions for a standard JAD/Design are discussed in the first section of this book. The topics of particular importance to the participants include the JAD/Design material (Chap. 2), the session and wrap-up material (Chap. 3), and the participant roles (Chap. 4). If tailoring of the process and outputs has occurred, the session leader incorporates the changes into the contents of the participant preparation package.

The way in which the session leader assists the participants to prepare for the session phase varies, depending on whether the participant is a user representative, an information systems representative, a specialist, or an analyst. Within the participant preparation package, the session leader requests that the user representatives and user specialists perform the following five preparation tasks:

1. Review the entire participant preparation package and note questions, concerns, and ideas they may have.
2. Gather, review, and bring to session any documentation they may have that describes the way they currently operate. This could include manuals, forms

they complete, reports they prepare for others, and reports others prepare for them.

3. Consult their colleagues for ideas on how the system could improve the way work is currently done.

4. Pay attention to the manner in which they use information as they currently work. Note problems, such as information not being available or difficulties in using the data they have.

5. Start a list of the data they would like to have available on the system.

Information systems representatives and information systems specialists are typically asked to perform the following three preparation tasks:

1. Review the entire participant preparation package and note questions, concerns, and ideas they may have.

2. Gather, review, and bring to session relevant data dictionary listings for any existing systems performing similar functions to the one being designed, as well as for systems that will interface with the system being designed.

3. Consider whether there are any hardware or software constraints or assumptions that affect the requirements and external design stage of the development life cycle. This often takes the form of investigating the maintenance and development status, capabilities, and needs of interfacing systems.

It follows that user and information systems representatives who participate in more than one JAD/Design will have less preparation to perform after having completed their first JAD/Design.

In addition to the information provided to the user and information systems representatives and specialists, the session leader provides the specialists with more specific details relevant to their participation. The specialists are told what area of expertise they are expected to contribute, approximately when they will participate, and for how long. They will also be briefed on the design work that has occurred in session prior to their participation. During JAD/Design customization, the session leader may only be able to provide the specialists with rough estimates of the duration and dates of their participation. Schedule adjustments may be needed as the session progresses and the participants make the design decisions that define in more detail the extent of the effort.

In many cases, the session leader must help the analysts prepare for the session phase as well. Ideally, the analysts will have had prior JAD/Design experience. However, they frequently are programmers who have had little exposure to the methodology. If this is the case, they should endeavor to gain as thorough an understanding of JAD as possible. A reading of Chaps. 1 through 10 of this book will provide them with the requisite information. They should then discuss and review the material with the session leader.

Once trained in the methodology, the analysts must coordinate with the session leader to determine the logistics of the documentation effort for the session phase. Which of the session results will the session leader record on flip charts or transparencies, alleviating the need for an analyst also to take notes? If there are two analysts, will they rotate actively recording the results? The session leader and analysts run through the session tasks and determine how each one will be handled.

TAILOR TASKS AND OUTPUTS

During the JAD/Plan customization phase, the JAD tasks and outputs were reviewed and tailored. The goal was to fit the standard JAD tasks and outputs to the organization and the specific project underway. However, as the project progresses and more information surfaces, the session leader focuses on each particular JAD/Design during its customization phase to determine if any more detailed tailoring or "tweaking" of the process or outputs is needed.

For example, during the orientation task for the SUPER system order processing and reporting JAD/Design, the vice president of sales reveals to the session leader that in his opinion management reporting may turn out to be a stumbling block for the JAD/Design session. Although all seem to be aware of the need for management summary reports to monitor and evaluate sales, they had never had such an overwhelming amount of data to manipulate before. He believes that the task of selecting which statistics should be on the standard production reports (as opposed to being available for analysis on an ad hoc basis) will be an arduous task.

After hearing this concern, the session leader decides to add a sixth requirements topic to this particular JAD/Design session. The participants will be asked to list the "key indicators" that help to gauge the success of a product or a sales territory. By directing the participants to identify these factors during the initial, more general stages of the session phase, the session leader hopes to keep them from getting bogged down in the details and overwhelmed by data later in the session. The key indicators flip chart will serve as a mind jogger and a guide to defining the management reports.

PREPARE MATERIALS FOR SESSION

During JAD/Design customization, materials preparation is typically the most time-consuming task. The purpose of materials preparation is to enable the session phase to run as smoothly and professionally as possible. The session leader and analyst(s) work together to

- Arrange for a session room, equipment, and supplies.
- Prepare visual aids and forms.
- Lay the groundwork for documentation and prototype efforts.
- Set up the session room.

Arrange for Session Room, Equipment, and Supplies

The session leader or one of the analysts coordinates with the appropriate individuals in order to arrange for the session room, equipment, and supplies. The first decision to be made is whether or not to hold the session off-site, such as in another organization-owned facility or in a local hotel. The major advantage to holding the session at a site other than the participants' primary work location is that the participants are less likely to be interrupted or distracted by the continuing demands of their jobs. In all cases, a conference room must be booked in advance of the session dates.

Session support equipment, such as an overhead projector, flip chart stands, and a magnetic board, must be scheduled. In addition, markers, flip chart paper, a spare overhead projector bulb, transparencies, JAD magnetics, and paper and pencils must be procured. Depending on the times of day that the session will be held, appropriate meals and/or refreshments may be requested.

Prepare Visual Aids and Forms

Figure 8-1 lists the typical visual aids and forms prepared for a JAD/Design session. The issues, considerations, agenda, and "welcome" flip charts are prepared for a JAD/Design in the same way as they are for a JAD/Plan (see Chap. 5).

- ✔ JAD Introductory Presentations
- ✔ Requirements and Scope Topics
- ✔ Screen Layout Forms
- ✔ Report Layout Forms
- ✔ Edit and Validation Forms
- ✔ Interface Description Forms
- ✔ Data Element Description Forms
- ✔ Function Description Forms
- ✔ Issues Forms
- ✔ Considerations
- ✔ Session Agenda
- ✔ "Welcome" Flip Chart (with system and JAD/Design name)

Figure 8-1   Visual aids to prepare for JAD/Design session.

JAD introductory presentation.   The session leader prepares two types of introductory presentations for the JAD/Design session. The first is an overview of the entire JAD methodology and JAD/Design outputs. This overview is presented to the participants as part of the session phase kickoff, before any design work begins. Its purpose is to provide the participants with a general understanding of what they will be doing during the course of the session phase and what the documentation and prototype outputs will look like.

The second introductory presentation reviews the JAD/Design tasks and outputs in more detail. The session leader will present the material explaining a given task just before the participants are to perform that task for the first time. For each JAD/Design session task, the session leader covers the task's purpose, how the task is to be accomplished, and how the outputs are to be formatted. Sample outputs help the participants to envision better what they are striving to achieve.

For the JAD/Design session task of designing screen and report layouts, the session leader provides additional background on screen and report design factors. This briefing includes a review of the layout size; standard header, footer, and message areas; cursor movement capabilities; and function key usage. It also presents considerations such as placing fields that are required on data entry at the top of the screen and trade-offs such as screen or report crowding versus paging (using more than one screen or report layout).

Requirements and scope.   The session leader and analysts prepare visual aids for the requirements and the JAD/Design scope (see Fig. 8-2). Each requirement and scope topic has a separate flip chart or transparency. The session leader and analysts place a heading at the top of the flip chart or transparency. They then extract relevant bullet-formatted text from their discussions during the orientation task and from previously completed project documents (i.e., the JAD/Plan document or, in the case of a multi-JAD/Design project, a prior JAD/Design

```
• Requirements Topics
     Objectives
     Anticipated benefits
     Strategic and future considerations
     Constraints and assumptions
     Security, audit, and control

• Scope Topics
     System users
     System locations
     In-scope (functional areas)
     Out-of-Scope (functional areas)
```

Figure 8-2   Requirements and scope topics.

document). During the JAD/Design session phase the participants will refine and expand upon these initial items, providing more detail for each topic.

In most cases, flip charts are used for these items so that, when completed in session, they may be hung on the walls and serve as mind joggers for the remainder of the session tasks. In many of our conference rooms, we have had to "wallpaper" every inch of available space with the flip charts in order to fit them all. In one instance we placed the out-of-scope flip chart on the ceiling to remind participants which areas were considered "blue sky," wish-list items. When the room does not accommodate the sole use of flip charts, a combination of flip charts and transparencies may be used. The flip charts are then reserved for the more significant items such as the scope.

Layout, edit and validation, and interface definition forms.   The session leader and analysts prepare numerous copies of "skeleton" or fill-in-the-blank transparencies for the screen and report layouts, edit and validation specifications, and interface definitions.[1] These formatted transparencies can then be completed in session with transparency markers. The session leader determines how many copies of each transparency type to make based on the estimates for the JAD/Design.

The screen and report layout transparencies have the standard header and footer or message areas completed and, in the case of a screen layout, indicate the line numbers of the screen (see Fig. 8-3(a) and 8-3(b)). The lines are usually double or triple spaced in order to be large enough for the session leader to complete with transparency markers.

The edit and validation transparencies are made up of an initial identification area followed by a body of four columns (see Fig. 8-4). The identification area leaves space for the session leader to fill in the function and screen names. The four columns are set up for the item number, data element name, use code, and edit and validation specifications.

The interface description transparencies are fill-in-the-blank types of forms (see Fig. 8-5). They provide areas to write the interface name, sending system, receiving system, estimated frequency of the interface, list of data elements included in the interface, and an area for special notes or comments about the interface.

Data element description and function description.   The analysts typically make paper copies of the data element description and function description formats (see Figs. 8-6 and 8-7). Although both of these formats are mostly fill-in-the-blank, each has an area for some narration. The data element description has space for a one- to two-sentence explanation of the data element. The function description format reserves a larger area for a narrative describing the function purpose and flow.

---

[1]In situations where transparencies are not possible, flip charts and paper copies are substituted for the transparencies.

SCREEN LAYOUT

Function Name:

Screen Name:

1	(TRANS ID)	** SUPER SYSTEM **	MM/DD/YY HH:MM:SS
2		(Screen title)	
3			
4			
5			
6			
7			
8			
9			
10			
11			
12			
13			
14			
15			
16			
17			
18			
19			
20			
21			
22			

23 and 24 reserved for system messages

Figure 8-3(a)   Screen layout form.

REPORT LAYOUT

Function Name:

Report Name:

(REPORT ID)		** SUPER SYSTEM **	(PAGE NO.)
(As of date)		(Report title)	(Run date)

Figure 8-3(b) Report layout form.

EDIT & VALIDATION			

Function Name:

Screen Name:

Use Codes: R = Required;   O = Optional
                        D = Displayed; P = Protected

Item No.	Abbreviated Name	Use Code	Edit/Validation

Figure 8-4 Edit and validation form..

Organize the forms.   The analysts and session leader organize their materials so that they can readily find both the formats on which they are taking the notes and the formats that they have completed. This applies equally to the paper and the transparency formats. Most people find it easiest to create a folder for each format type (e.g., one for data element descriptions, another for edit and validation specifications), as well as for the completed formats. During the session they can quickly find any given format by reaching into the appropriate folder.

INTERFACE DESCRIPTION

Interface Name:

System From:

System To:

Estimated Frequency:

Data Elements:

Notes:

Figure 8-5   Interface description form.

Lay the Groundwork for Documentation and Prototype Efforts

The third aspect of materials preparation is laying the groundwork for the documentation and prototype efforts. The analysts with guidance from the session leader, set up the automated documentation environment for the particular JAD/

DATA ELEMENT DESCRIPTION

Full Name:

Abbreviated Name:

Size:

Data Type: (9 = numeric; A = alphabetic; X = alphanumeric)

Format:

Description:

Values, Ranges, Comments:

Figure 8-6   Data element description form.

Design. The session leader also helps the information systems representatives to set up the prototype environment.

Documentation is usually accomplished via one of two strategies. Organizations use generalized word or document processing software or they tailor JAD in order to use computer-aided software engineering (CASE) packages.

When an organization takes the more generalized documentation package

---

FUNCTION DESCRIPTION

Function Name:

Estimated Volume:

Function Narrative:

Security/Distribution:

_____   _____

_____   _____

_____   _____

_____   _____

_____   _____

_____   _____

_____   _____

Figure 8-7 Function description form.

route, the analysts put the JAD/Design documentation formats onto the system. During wrap-up they will be able to copy any given format and fill in the information on the copy. This approach saves time because the basic format is only typed once and is merely copied for each use. Having the analysts work from a standard set of formats also helps to ensure document consistency.

Regardless of whether the documentation system is generalized or specific to software design, logistics must be determined for the documentation and prototype software's use during the JAD/Design effort. This includes such considerations as establishing file naming conventions, ensuring that there is sufficient storage space, and implementing backup procedures for the files. In situations where the information systems representative will develop the prototype, he or she should coordinate with the session leader and analysts on this task.

Set Up Session Room

The session room is usually set up during the afternoon prior to the session phase. The session leader and analysts arrange the seating, hang the flip charts, and set up the overhead projector, magnetic board, and the automated documentation system, if used in session.

The session leader and analysts determine the best seating arrangement based on the room size and number of participants. A typical JAD/Design room layout is shown in Fig. 8-8. The participants are seated in a horseshoe arrangement, which accommodates a fairly large group of people and allows them to see and hear each other. For smaller groups, seating around a conference table may also be effective.

The visual aids are placed so that they are easily viewed given the seating arrangement chosen. When hanging flip charts on the walls, it is advisable to place blank sheets of paper directly underneath. Some of the markers bleed through standard flip chart paper. Better to stain the backup sheets than the conference room walls. Whenever possible, a nonglare surface should be planned for projecting the transparencies. Effectively placed visual aids provide participants with readily accessible reference points and mind joggers during the session phase.

TO TAPE OR NOT TO TAPE THE SESSION

It is frequently suggested that session discussions be tape recorded in order to assist the analysts in their documentation effort. I discourage this for two reasons.

First, a tape recorder has a tendency to inhibit discussion. Some individuals will be less likely to ask questions or to voice their opinions knowing that others within the organization can at a later time replay the discussion. Even those participants who have no qualms about openly expressing their viewpoints may refrain from divulging delicate or sensitive information if the session is being taped. One type of situation where the presence of a tape recorder inhibits open discussion arises when the system design involves the implementation of organizational policies. With the tape recorder in the room, everyone will merely recite the organizational policy, the party line. Without the tape recorder, people will talk frankly about how and why the policy is currently circumvented. This type of information is important to discuss if the system is to be effective.

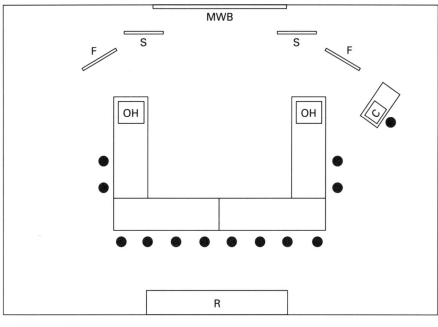

Key:
● = Participant
C = Computer system / terminal
F = Flip-chart stands
MWB = Magnetic writing board
OH = Overhead projector
R = Refreshments
S = Screens / projection surface

Figure 8-8   Sample session room arrangement.

For example, in our SUPER system, the system will have to incorporate the company's policy regarding transferring existing customer accounts among sales territories (i.e., regions, branch offices). Customers and all of their orders are supposed to be transferred to a different sales territory whenever the customer or its purchasing department relocates to a different geographic territory. Considerable incentive currently exists for a sales territory to hide or "overlook" (as the sales representatives put it) the need to transfer a good customer, at least until the beginning of a new quota year. In the meantime, the sales force does not adequately cover the customer due to the geographic separation and the knowledge that the customer will eventually be transferred to another territory anyway.

By discussing such issues openly in session, the participants may discover that the reason for the policy of transferring all of the open orders at the time of customer transfer is merely to avoid the overwhelming amount of manual processing required to associate a customer with a different territory than his backlog. Had they never discussed the realities of the policy, the participants would have designed the system to reflect the status quo. Instead, they can now help to revise the policy and design the system to be more equitable to the sales territories. This will also result in better customer service.

My second argument against tape recording is that it is unnecessary to the documentation effort. Most of the JAD/Design is documented via diagram, fill-in-the-blank forms, or bullet-formatted text. Rarely do the analysts take dictation of more than three or four sentences at a time. The session leader usually assists the analysts by recording some of the decisions on preformatted flip charts and transparencies. In fact, if the analysts were to rely on the taped material, they would add considerable time to the documentation effort. During wrap-up, they would have to run through all of the taped discussions in order to extract the appropriate output.

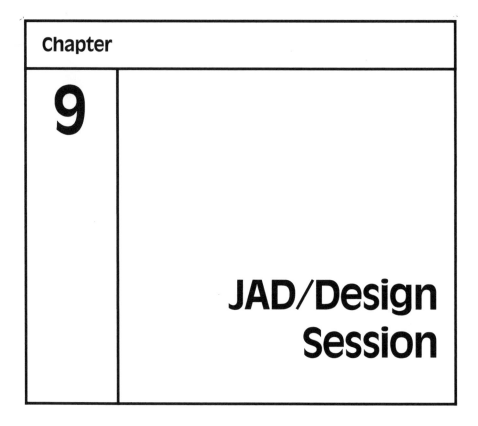

Chapter

9

JAD/Design Session

The JAD/Design session phase is much like the last, steep stretch of a hike up a mountain. This part of the climb is the essence of the entire effort, culminating in the exhilarating feeling of reaching the summit. All of the other JAD activities are geared either toward getting to this point—planning and preparing for the JAD/Design session—or toward returning and relating the accomplishment to others.

Throughout the JAD/Design session, the participants exert a tremendous amount of effort and creativity. They refine and expand upon the high-level requirements defined during the JAD/Plan session. They then design the system from the users' point of view, specifying exactly what they want the system to do and to display.

Prior to the commencement of a JAD/Design session, considerable work has been accomplished. The JAD/Plan activity has been completed, setting out the high-level requirements for the system, defining the JAD/Design scope, planning the JAD/Design, and publishing the results. The JAD/Design customization phase has also been completed. During customization, the session leader, analysts, and other participants prepared for the JAD/Design session. In the case of multi-JAD/Design projects, other JAD/Design(s) focusing on other subsystems may have been completed as well.

Whereas the JAD/Plan participants typically are executives, managers, and other key employees who provide a fairly high-level perspective of the business, participants in the JAD/Design are a much more mixed group. They are selected during the JAD/Plan session to collectively cover the knowledge base required by the JAD/Design scope. The JAD/Design session participant list usually includes a number of user representatives, one or more information systems representatives, and one or more specialists. The session leader facilitates the session and the analysts help to record the results.

Strictly speaking, the executive sponsor is available on an as-needed basis during the session phase but does not participate full time in the session discussions. However, the individual filling the executive sponsor role may also play the role of a user representative or a specialist. This type of dual assignment is appropriate in situations where the executive will be a user of the system (see Chap. 4).

In the example of the SUPER system sales management JAD/Design, the vice president of sales is both the executive sponsor and a major user of the system. He will participate in the sales management JAD/Design session full time as a user representative. However, during the SUPER system order processing and reporting JAD/Design, he will fill only his executive sponsor role.

During the JAD/Plan session, the JAD/Designs are estimated and scheduled. The JAD/Design scopes are adjusted with the goal of keeping each JAD/Design session phase within three to ten workdays. Over the course of the session, the session leader guides the participants through the following tasks:[1]

- Conduct orientation.
- Review and refine JAD/Plan requirements and scope.
- Develop workflow diagram.
- Develop workflow description.
- Identify system data groups and functions.
- Design screen and report functions.
- Specify processing requirements.
- Define interface requirements.
- Document issues and considerations.
- Conclude session phase.

---

[1]These tasks are sometimes categorized. That is, the requirements, workflow, and function identification tasks are categorized as *system definition* tasks. The remaining tasks are categorized as *system design* tasks. These categories are purely conceptual and are completely transparent during the JAD/Design session.

CONDUCT ORIENTATION

The Kickoff

The purpose of orientation during the JAD/Design session phase is to increase the JAD/Design participants' understanding of the project history and the JAD methodology. Much of the orientation is accomplished during an initial kickoff presentation. The executive sponsor and the session leader coordinate their efforts to make the presentation both informational and motivational. They provide participants with project and JAD background information and motivate them to contribute their skills, knowledge, and initiative to the project as a team.

The executive sponsor usually begins the kickoff presentation by welcoming everyone to the session and providing a short history of the project. He or she gives the participants an appreciation for the importance of the project, what events have occurred to date, and the expectations the organization has set for the group. The executive sponsor usually reviews the business flow diagram in order to explain the JAD/Plan participants' perspective of the system. In the case of a multi-JAD/Design project, he or she highlights the area to be addressed during the current JAD/Design. The session leader then presents a general overview of the JAD methodology, avoiding too many details at this time.

Explaining the JAD Details

The details of the JAD/Design session are presented gradually within the course of the session. The session leader provides the participants with an orientation to each new task as they are about to perform that task for the first time. These task orientations vary in length from a brief explanation about refining the JAD/Plan requirements and scope items to as much as a 20-minute presentation on screen and report design. Sample outputs help the participants to envision better what they are striving to achieve.

REVIEW AND REFINE JAD/PLAN REQUIREMENTS AND SCOPE

New Participants, New Perspective

The JAD/Design participants begin their effort by adding detail to the requirements and scope items that were first defined during the JAD/Plan session. Whereas during the JAD/Plan session the participants had a fairly high-level perspective of the system, the JAD/Design participants are more familiar with the details. They add more refined features to the JAD/Plan responses.

In defining the requirements, the JAD/Design participants are forced to step away from their current view of operations and reexamine the system objectives.

This helps to avoid the frequently encountered downfall of expending the effort and cost of a new system that is merely a slight variation on the current one. By rethinking the system target, the participants begin to look in a more innovative, future-oriented direction.

Completing the Topics

During JAD/Design customization, the session leader and analysts prepared flip charts or transparencies for the JAD/Design session. They reviewed the JAD/Plan document and extracted bullet-formatted responses pertaining to the JAD/Design area. In the case of a multi-JAD/Design project, the JAD/Design area constitutes a subsystem; in the case of a single JAD/Design project, it encompasses the entire system. The session leader and analysts placed the bullet items on the appropriate visual aids for each of the requirements and scope topics.

During the JAD/Design session, the session leader asks the participants to address each of the topics individually. The requirements topics include objectives, anticipated benefits, strategic and future considerations, constraints and assumptions, as well as security, audit, and control requirements. The scope topics include JAD/Design users, locations, and in-scope and out-of-scope items (functional areas).

The session leader identifies the current topic, reviews the existing responses for that topic, and encourages the participants to contribute their ideas. As the participants voice their thoughts, the session leader or analyst writes them in bullet format on the flip charts or transparencies that were prepared during JAD/Design customization. The participants then evaluate and refine the responses. As the participants discuss and make decisions about the requirements and scope topics, they begin to lay a foundation of agreement upon which they continue to build.

When the session leader and participants are satisfied that the current topic has been fully covered, the next topic for discussion is identified. Refinements to previous topics may be made at any time.

DEVELOP WORKFLOW DIAGRAM

Why Use a Workflow Diagram?

The workflow diagram illustrates how the system fits within the context of the organization's overall operations and how the organization will accomplish its work under the new system (see Fig. 9-1). It provides more detail about the scope of the system than does the JAD/Plan business flow diagram (refer to Chap. 6). Rather than comprising the fairly high-level procedures of the business flow diagram, the workflow diagram consists of smaller functional pieces, termed *processes*.

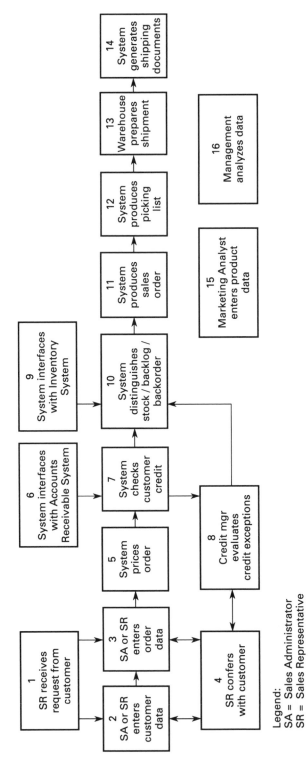

Figure 9-1 Sample workflow diagram.

Legend:
SA = Sales Administrator
SR = Sales Representative

Generate Process Magnetics

A process may reflect manual functions, system functions, or interfaces with other systems. Whereas a JAD/Plan procedure is expressed in general terms as a verb and an object, a JAD/Design process is specified more explicitly, usually as a subject, verb, and object (who? acts upon? what?). Examples of SUPER system processes include "Sales Administrator or Sales Rep Enters Order Data," "System Produces Sales Order," and "System Interfaces with Accounts Receivable System."

The session leader encourages the participants to list all of the processes that are to be included in the JAD/Design scope area. The processes are those for the new system environment, reflecting the defined requirements and scope rather than the current way of operating. It is often easiest for the participants to think of the processes sequentially, beginning with one of the initial events and generating ideas about what should happen next. As the participants contribute their ideas, the session leader or analyst writes each process onto its own erasable vinyl magnetic card (the 5.0-inch by 7.5-inch process blocks) and places the magnetics on a magnetic board.

Diagram with Magnetics

Once the participants conclude that they have identified most if not all of the processes, they are asked to come to the magnetic board and arrange the process magnetics in the design of a workflow diagram. The participants draw the connecting arrows onto the magnetic board with erasable dry markers. The goal is to depict the general flow(s) of system use. Processes that do not fit well into the general flow(s) are inserted on one side of the diagram but not connected by arrows to any other processes. In the SUPER system order processing and reporting JAD/Design, "Management Analyzes Data" and "Marketing Analyst Enters Product Data" are examples of such processes.

When new ideas arise, the changes to the processes and arrows are easily and neatly accommodated by the erasable magnetic media. The participants may attempt various alternatives, each one triggering constructive, thoughtful discussion.

When the participants are satisfied with their workflow diagram, the session leader asks them to critique the diagram in light of the requirements and scope topics. Is the system that the workflow diagram represents a truly effective solution to the requirements? Can all of the requirements be met by this solution? Does the workflow diagram's scope match that set forth by the scope topics? As a result of this analysis, the participants may decide to make further adjustments to the workflow diagram, requirements, and/or scope topics.

At this point, the workflow diagram is still on the erasable, movable magnetic medium. Once finalized, it must be copied onto a more permanent visual aid. The analyst can copy the diagram onto a transparency while the session leader introduces the participants to the next task. As it is being copied, each process block is assigned a sequential identification number to be used for cross-referencing to the workflow description.

DEVELOP WORKFLOW DESCRIPTION

The workflow description elaborates on each process included in the workflow diagram, bringing the system definition down to a lower level of detail (see Fig. 9-2). In doing so, the description enforces more discipline on the JAD/Design participants' thought process, helps to cross-educate the participants, and eventually helps the readers of the JAD/Design document to better understand the system design.

Disciplines the Analytical Process

The workflow description requires the JAD/Design participants to discuss further and define each process in the workflow diagram. By delving into each process, the participants consider all of its implications in light of the new system

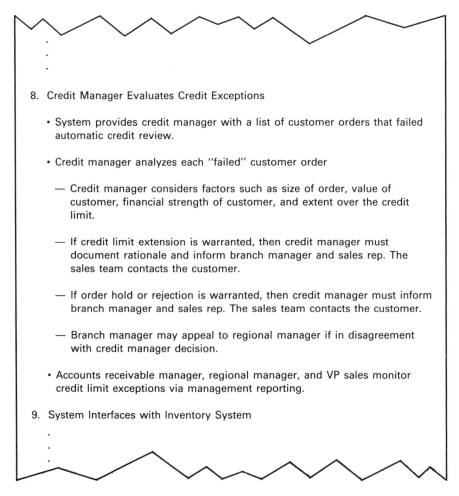

8. Credit Manager Evaluates Credit Exceptions

    • System provides credit manager with a list of customer orders that failed automatic credit review.

    • Credit manager analyzes each "failed" customer order

      — Credit manager considers factors such as size of order, value of customer, financial strength of customer, and extent over the credit limit.

      — If credit limit extension is warranted, then credit manager must document rationale and inform branch manager and sales rep. The sales team contacts the customer.

      — If order hold or rejection is warranted, then credit manager must inform branch manager and sales rep. The sales team contacts the customer.

      — Branch manager may appeal to regional manager if in disagreement with credit manager decision.

    • Accounts receivable manager, regional manager, and VP sales monitor credit limit exceptions via management reporting.

9. System Interfaces with Inventory System

Figure 9-2 Sample workflow description.

environment. This is the stage in the design process when the participants typically discuss exception situations, ingrained assumptions, existing organizational policies, and new policy requirements—critical but often overlooked aspects of system design. For example, in discussing the process "Credit Manager Evaluates Credit Exceptions" for the SUPER system order processing and reporting JAD/Design, the participants reflect on the degree of authority to grant the credit managers, what role, if any, the branch office managers should have in determining whether to extend a customer's credit limit, as well as what audit and control precautions should be implemented to safeguard the credit extension process.

Cross-Educates Participants

The second purpose of the workflow description is to cross-educate the participants. As the participants define each process in detail, they often educate each other about unfamiliar areas of the organization. Although each of the participants was chosen for a particular area of expertise, a participant knowledgeable in all areas is the rare exception. Not only does this shared knowledge enable the participants to generate better, more appropriate ideas, but it also decreases the potential amount of conflict and disagreement among the participants later in the session. Many of the disagreements in session stem from differences in the participants' perception or understanding of a given situation. Once the participants arrive at a common perspective, they are more likely to derive similar conclusions.

Communicates System Context

The workflow description is also an invaluable section of the eventual JAD/ Design document. After the JAD/Design session is completed and time passes, the participants may forget many of the assumptions and decisions they made in session. In addition, many individuals who did not participate in the JAD/Design may need to learn about the system. In particular, the technical team that will be developing the system must rely on the JAD/Design document to become educated about the new system. The workflow description provides them with much of the information they need in order to understand the system context.

Generating the Workflow Description

The session leader guides the participants through the task of developing the workflow description, examining each process individually. He or she identifies the current process for discussion within the workflow diagram and writes the process name and its sequential number on a transparency or flip chart.

The participants then generate bullet-formatted description for the process. They provide information about who is involved in the process, the events that may occur, and what the process produces. They also record exception situations that are not explicitly depicted in the workflow diagram. The session leader writes the bullet items on the visual aid underneath the process name. When the session leader and

```
┌──────────────────────────────────────────────────────────────────────┐
│                        LIST OF DATA GROUPS                             │
│                                                                        │
│   Data Group              Description                                  │
│   ─────────               ───────────                                  │
│   • Customer Data         Data pertaining to those organizations or    │
│                           individuals who currently have open orders   │
│                           or who have placed order(s) in the past.     │
│                                                                        │
│   • Order Data            Data pertaining to a specific customer       │
│                           request to purchase products.               │
│                                                                        │
│   • Product Data          Data pertaining to complete products and     │
│                           components that are offered for sale to      │
│                           customers.                                   │
│                                                                        │
└───╱╲────╱╲╱╲──────╱╲───╱╲────╱╲──────╱╲───╱╲───────╱╲─────────────────┘
```

Figure 9-3 Sample list of data groups.

participants are satisfied that the process has been completed, the session leader identifies the next process to be described.

IDENTIFY SYSTEM DATA GROUPS AND FUNCTIONS

Develop List of Data Groups

Once the workflow diagram and description have been defined, the session leader asks the participants to develop a list of data groups that identifies the categories of data elements that the system must store (see Fig. 9-3). The data groups add one more dimension or layer to the system definition. Whereas the participants examined the system from a functional or processing viewpoint in developing the workflows, they now turn their attention to the entities that the system will store and manipulate.

Although a database designer may be a JAD/Design session participant, the task here is not to create a database design or even to adhere to strict database standards in defining segments or tables. Rather, the goal is to identify *logical* data groups that have meaning to the users. The database designer will eventually create a database or file design as a separate, technical task later in the software development life cycle.[2]

---

[2] Some organizations have tailored the JAD/Design to take the data analysis one step farther. After developing a list of data groups, the participants create an entity-relationship diagram. This type of diagram contains all of the entities with arrows showing which entities are directly related to one another. The arrowheads show whether there is a single or multiple relationship—for example, that a customer may have more than one order, but an order may only have one customer. A product may be on many orders and an order may have many products.

The session leader asks the participants to list the data groups that the system will store. The requirements, scope, workflow diagram and workflow description serve as mind joggers to the participants, helping them to generate a complete list.

The session leader then asks the participants to develop a brief definition for each data group. Although in many cases, this exercise may seem superfluous, particularly to the user representatives familiar with the terminology, it is often extremely helpful to those individuals who require orientation to the system's terminology, such as the technical team. In addition, the data group definition often helps to clarify assumptions even for the seasoned user. For example, the SUPER system definition of product data explicitly states that it encompasses data pertaining to salable components as well as to completed products.

Develop List of System Functions

Once the participants have completed the list of data groups, they begin the task of generating a list of system functions. JAD uses the word *function* in referring to the smallest functional piece within a system's external design. A JAD function usually equates to a low-level option on the system's menu. "Add Product Data," "Generate Sales Order," and "Interface from Accounts Receivable" are all considered JAD functions. The purpose of the list of system functions is to set the agenda for the remainder of the JAD/Design session. It identifies each screen, report, processing routine, and interface that the participants must design before the close of the session phase.

The session leader once more guides the participants through the workflow diagram and description, asking them to identify which functions the system must perform in order to accomplish or support each process. As the participants generate ideas and make their decisions, the session leader or analyst writes the functions named on a flip chart or transparency.

Some workflow processes will not require any system functions, as in the case of the SUPER system process "Sales Rep Confers with Customer." These are purely manual processes. Some workflow processes will translate into a single function or a set of functions.[3] For example, the SUPER system process "Sales Administrator or Sales Rep Enters Customer Data" translates into the set of functions "Add, Change, Delete, View Customer Data." Other workflow processes will translate into multiple functions. The SUPER system process "Credit Manager Evaluates Credit Exceptions" generates the functions "View Credit Exceptions Summary," "Add, Change, Delete, View Exception Credit Evaluation," and "Credit Evaluation Summary Report."

After the participants have completed the review of the workflow processes and have generated a preliminary list of system functions, they evaluate the list against the list of data groups. Their goal is to ensure that the list of system

---

[3]An example of a set of functions would be "Add, Change, Delete, View Customer Data." Each of these four functions uses the same screen layout(s). However, the edit and validation requirements will vary, as will such function description items as security requirements and estimated volumes.

functions provides for the input, processing, and output of all of the data groups. In examining the list of system functions from both the processing and data group viewpoints, the participants help to control the completeness and quality of their design.[4]

At this point, the task of generating the list of system functions is considered complete. The list of system functions now becomes the "to-do" list or agenda for the remainder of the JAD/Design session phase.

The session leader guides the participants through the list, asking them to complete the design of one function before proceeding to the next one. The input-oriented functions are usually sequenced first, reserving the output-oriented reports and inquiries for the end. Ordering the functions in this way seems more natural for the participants' thought process and helps in the identification of data elements (see the discussion on identifying data elements in the next section).

As the participants design the details of each function, they may decide to make alterations to the function list. They may recognize the need for an additional function, realize that two functions could be better accomplished as one, or decide to modify the scope of an existing function.

DESIGN SCREEN AND REPORT FUNCTIONS

The session leader guides the participants through the following series of tasks to design each screen and report function:

- Identify data elements.
- Design screen or report layout.
- Specify edit and validation requirements (screen functions only).
- Complete the function description.

Identify Data Elements

The session leader begins the discussion of a screen or report function by ensuring that all of the participants understand which screen or report is being discussed. The participants review where the function fits within the workflow and what purpose it will serve. The session leader then asks the participants to name all of the data elements that should be included on the screen or report. A data element is a specific piece of data, also known as a "field." "Customer Name," "Product Number," and "Order Date" are examples of data elements.

As the participants identify a data element for the first time within the system, they also define a number of characteristics about that piece of data. Characteristics include the full and abbreviated names, the size, data type, format, description, and

---

[4]The one type of function that often escapes this analysis is the menu function(s). The session leader often has to suggest that menus be added to the bottom of the list of system functions.

comments/possible values. The analyst captures all of the information about the data element on a data element description form (see Fig. 9-4).

Data element description purpose. The purpose of the data element description form is to provide a central repository for all static information about each data element. As purely a text form, the data element description may be used

---

DATA ELEMENT DESCRIPTION

Full Name: Order Entry Date

Abbreviated Name: Entry Date

Size: 6

Data Type: 9   (9 = numeric; A = alphabetic; X = alphanumeric)

Format: Valid Date, mm/dd/yy

Description: The date on which an order is originally entered into the system.

Values, Ranges, Comments: (not applicable)

Figure 9-4   Sample data element description.

as a reference to look up information easily about any given data element. It facilitates the task of incorporating any changes to the information during the design process. Software design packages that provide more sophisticated data dictionary features often help with cross-references between data elements and their usage and can eventually expedite the technical database design task.

Data element names.   The participants define both a full name for the data element and a standard abbreviation that will appear on all of the screens and reports. This abbreviation is *not* a programmer's name for the data. Eventually, the technical team will develop a separate data element name to be used within the programs. It is, instead, an abbreviation that will be used consistently on all of the system externals so that the users may more easily learn and understand the system.

Data element size.   In specifying the data element size, the participants are asked for the maximum length of the data element (i.e., the largest number of characters/digits acceptable). Knowing the length will enable the participants to design screens and reports to accommodate the data and will also provide the technical team with the information it needs to program the system.

Data type.   The data type refers to whether the data are alphabetic, numeric, or a mixture, known as alphanumeric. The data type is important to the technical team and helps to ensure data integrity by enforcing some constraints on the combination of characters, symbols, and digits that are entered and stored in the data element. The participants identify the data element's data type, which is recorded by the analyst on the data element description form.

Data format.   Although most data elements do not have a specific format or pattern, elements such as dates and certain codes often do. For example, dates are often specified as mm/dd/yy. Whenever a data element does have a format, the format is specified on the data element description form.

Description.   The description area is used to define the data in the user's terms. One of the participants usually dictates one or two sentences that explain the meaning of the data element. The description is particularly helpful in distinguishing data elements with similar but not synonymous meanings and in making explicit some of the potentially confusing aspects of the data element. For example, the descriptions for the SUPER system will highlight the difference between ''order date'' (the date on which the customer signs the order) and ''order entry date'' (the date on which the order is originally entered into the system).

Comments/possible values.   The comments/possible values section of the data element description form is primarily used to specify ranges within which the data must fall, possible coded values as well as any miscellaneous notes about the data element. For example, the data element ''order terms'' (abbreviated

Figure 9-5 Sample data element magnetic. The abbreviated name of the data element is written on the left of the data element magnetic. The number of spaces needed to display the abbreviated name is written in the upper right of the magnetic and the number of spaces for the element is written in the lower right. In the case of data elements that have intrinsic formatting characters, such as the slashes in dates, the data element size listed on the magnetic will be different from the size specified on the data element description form. Although it is customary to omit the intrinsic formatting characters from the data element description size, they are always included in the magnetic size since they will require space when displayed on a screen or report.

"terms") will have a list of valid values that will be specified on the data element description form.[5]

Record new data elements. As the participants define the new data element and the analyst records the information on the data element description form, the session leader writes the data element's abbreviated name, the abbreviated name size, and the data element size on an erasable vinyl magnetic card (see Fig. 9-5). Both the size of the abbreviated name and the size of the data element indicate the number of spaces required for display on a screen or report. The magnetic card serves three major purposes.

Magnetics facilitate layout design. The magnetics facilitate the design of screen and report layouts. The participants will be able to move the magnetics around on the board easily to design the layouts. They can try out as many ideas as they like before developing a consensus around a final solution and committing the result to a transparency. When determining whether all of the data elements will fit on a particular line of the layout, the data element sizing information is used for easy reference.

Magnetics maintain consistency. The magnetic card helps to maintain consistency throughout the JAD/Design process. Before we used data element magnetics, it was often a tedious and imprecise task to recall the standard abbreviated name and size for a data element from one screen or report design to the next. It

[5]It is not uncommon for the participants to feel that a new type of coded data element will require a separate task force to develop the possible codes. As long as the participants can decide on the size and data type of the coding scheme (e.g., that it will be a two-digit numeric code), they may place a comment on the data element description form to the effect that the coding scheme must be developed as a separate effort. This will also generate a consideration, identifying the need for the data element's coding scheme.

was considerably more difficult to maintain consistency among JAD/Designs in a multi-JAD/Design project. The analyst always had to look up the abbreviated name and size on the handwritten data element description forms, bogging down the process. Worse still, when participants relied solely on their memory for the information, the technical team eventually had to sort out whether such elements as "order number," "Order No," "Order Num," and "Ord No"—all found on different screens and reports—were distinct elements or merely a result of sloppy design.

When data element magnetics are utilized, consistency is easily maintained. The first time a data element is included in a system function, the participants provide all of the data element description information and the session leader writes up a magnetic card. The participants use the magnetic to design the layout, the agreed-upon layout is copied onto a transparency, and the session leader collects all of the magnetics for later use.[6] In subsequent functions that call for the data element, the session leader merely places the already created magnetic up on the board. There is no need for relying on memory or searching other sources for information about the data element.

What this approach implies is that the initial few functions for most JAD/Design sessions usually take longer to accomplish than the subsequent functions. Once most of the data elements have been defined, the participants merely name a data element and place the magnetic on the board.

Magnetics ensure thorough design.   The third purpose for utilizing data element magnetics is to prevent displaying or otherwise utilizing data elements that are not contained in the system. The magnetics help to ensure that data elements required on an output (e.g., presented on a screen or a report) have been previously created as part of another function, or are being calculated based on existing data elements or constants in the system.

The session leader usually sequences the functions so that the input-oriented functions are designed first. The magnetics are therefore created when the data element is first introduced in the system. When the data element is required for an output or in processing, the existence of a magnetic confirms that the element has in fact already been created. In cases where the data element first occurs in session while designing an output function, the session leader notes the need to create the data element under the appropriate function on the list of system functions. If the data element is to be created in a function covered within another JAD/Design, it is documented as a consideration.

Design Screen or Report Layout

Once the participants have identified all of the data elements for a given screen or report function and the session leader has placed the data element magnetics on the board, the group tackles the task of designing the screen or report

---

[6]When numerous magnetics have been defined, I find it helpful to keep the magnetics in alphabetic groupings to ease the task of finding any particular one.

layout. The session leader asks a few participants to come to the board to move the magnetics in the design of the layout.

Why design the layout?   Designing the layouts is a step that many other methodologies assign to the information systems department as part of the technical effort. However, this is an effort that takes little time, is enjoyed by the users, and contributes significantly to the design quality. Having the users design their own layouts also solidifies participant ownership of the design.

The higher quality of user-designed layouts results from the participants' intimate knowledge of the intended uses for the layouts. They understand all of the nuances and exception situations and can provide for them in the design. In addition, as the participants discuss a given screen or report and begin to move the data elements, they frequently refine their original list of data elements. This typically takes the form of adding to the layout data elements that were originally overlooked. The second reason for having the participants design their own layouts is to solidify their ownership of the design. They provide tangible input into the design; when they see the layouts in the JAD/Design document, prototype, and eventual system, they will recognize those layouts as their own.

As the participants begin to consider where to place the data element magnetics for a given function, they may recognize that there are too many data elements for one layout. They may choose to create multiple layouts, or pages, in order to accomplish the one function. For example, in the case of the SUPER system order processing and reporting JAD/Design, the participants decide that the amount and nature of the data for the function "Add an Order" warrants three layouts. The participants cluster the header, identification information on the first layout (see Fig. 9-6), the order line items on the second layout (e.g., products, prices), and specialty product specifications on a third layout.

Finalize the output.   When all of the data elements have been assigned a place on the layout, the session leader helps the participants to evaluate the design. He or she prompts the participants with questions based on the screen and report design presentation (see Chap. 8). The participants make refinements to the layout when necessary and reach a consensus on a solution. The resulting layout is then copied onto a transparency for future reference.

Multiple layout uses.   In situations where a set of screen functions is being designed (e.g., add, change, delete, view), the participants typically need only to identify data elements and design the layouts for the first function in the set. For the subsequent functions, the session leader displays the previously completed layouts on the overhead projector. The participants review the layouts and then continue with the remainder of the screen function tasks.

In the case of the SUPER system set of functions add, change, delete, and view an order, the layouts designed for the function add an order will be utilized for the other three functions in the set. However, the participants will define different

SCREEN LAYOUT

Function Name: Add an Order

Screen Name: Order Identification

```
           1111111111222222222233333333334444444444555555555566666666667777777778
  1234567890123456789012345678901234567890123456789012345678901234567890
 1 XXXXXXX              ** SUPER SYSTEM **              MM/DD/YY HH:MM:SS
 2                 ADD AN ORDER: ORDER IDENTIFICATION              1 OF 3
 3
 4 Order No:        S/Rep ID:          Order Date:
 5
 6 Cust No:         Cust. Name:
 7
 8 Cust Ref:                           Entry Date:
 9
10 SHIP TO INFORMATION:
11    Dept:
12    Street:                          PO:
13    City:                     State:    Zip:
14    Attn:
15
16    FOB:            Via:             Terms:
17
18 BILL TO INFORMATION:
19    Dept:
20    Street:                          PO:
21    City:                     State:    Zip:
22
23 (reserved for messages)
24 (reserved for messages)
```

Figure 9-6   Sample screen layout.

edit and validation requirements, as well as distinct function description material for the change, delete, and view functions.

Specify Edit and Validation Requirements

The participants define edit and validation requirements for each screen layout in a function. The edit and validation form becomes a backup sheet to a function's screen layouts, specifying how the system will handle the data on the screen (see Fig. 9-7).

The JAD/Design participants discuss each data element on the layout individually for edit and validation requirements. The session leader identifies the current data element on the screen layout, proceeding from left to right, top to bottom through the screen. The participants are asked to specify each data element's use and decide on the appropriate editing or validating that the system should perform. Typically either the analyst documents the decisions on an edit and validation hard

---

EDIT & VALIDATION

Function Name: Add an Order

Screen Name: Order Identification
(Screen 1 of 3)

Use Codes: R = Required;   O = Optional
D = Displayed;   P = Protected

Item No.	Abbreviated Name	Use Code	Edit/Validation
1	Order No	P	System generated Sequential number
2	S/Rep ID	R	Validated for match in system table
3	Order Date	R	Prior or equal to Entry Date (system date)
4	Cust No	R	Validated for match in customer file
5	Cust Name*	P	
6	Cust Ref	O	
7	Entry Date	P	System date
8	Ship to Dept*	D	
9	Ship to Street*	D	
10	Ship to PO*	D	
11	Ship to City*	D	May not be blank
12	Ship to State*	D	May not be blank. Validated for match in system table
(continued)			

Figure 9-7   Sample edit and validation.

EDIT & VALIDATION

Function Name: Add an Order

Screen Name: Order Identification
                       (Screen 1 of 3)

Use Codes: R = Required;   O = Optional
                       D = Displayed; P = Protected

Item No.	Abbreviated Name	Use Code	Edit/Validation
13	Ship to Zip*	D	Validated for match in system table
14	Ship to Attn*	D	
15	FOB	D	Defaults to "Shipping Point"
16	Via*	D	
17	Terms	D	Defaults to "Net 30." Must be valid value (see D/E Description)
18	Bill to Dept*	D	
19	Bill to Street*	D	
20	Bill to PO*	D	
21	Bill to City*	D	May not be blank
22	Bill to State*	D	May not be blank. Validated for match in system table
23	Bill to Zip*	D	Validated for match in system table

*Note that in these cases, customer data (e.g., Customer Ship to Department) is displayed; the confirmed or changed data are stored as Order data (e.g., Order Ship to Department).

Figure 9-7 *(Continued).*

copy form or the session leader writes the decisions on an edit and validation transparency form.

Identification information.   As the session leader identifies the current data element on the layout, the element is assigned a sequential item number, which is written on the edit and validation form along with the element's abbreviated name.

Use code.   The session leader then asks the participants to designate a use code for the data element. The codes are as follows:

R = Required. Upon data entry, the system will require users to place data into the data element. Users will not be allowed to skip over this element.

O = Optional. Upon data entry, the system will give the users the choice as to whether or not to place data into the data element. Users will be allowed to skip over this element.

D = Displayed. The system will present the data currently stored or calculated and will permit the user to change it or leave it as is.

P = Protected. The system will present the data currently stored or calculated and will not allow the users to make any changes.

Validation requirements.   For all data elements that are not protected (i.e., for R, O, and D), the participants determine the validation requirements. They decide what the system must do to ensure that the user enters valid data onto the screen. They may specify such validations as comparing the entered data against values in a file or system table, comparing the data with other data entered on the screen, or determining whether the data are within a certain range of values or calculations.

Sometimes the participants will want a displayed or protected data element (i.e., use codes of D or P) to present a calculated value to the user. In cases where the calculation is simple to express, such as a sum or a percentage, the participants specify the calculation in the validation area of the edit and validation form. More complex calculations and validations are specified as processing requirements (see the discussion of specifying processing requirements task). It is customary to place a cross-reference on the edit and validation form when a validation or calculation that affects a screen layout is documented on a processing requirements sheet.

Validations that reflect the data element description information of data element size, type, and format are usually not placed on the edit and validation form. The intent is to limit the occurrences of the same information within the document and thus simplify document updates and reduce the chance of error. In the case of data elements that have codes or value ranges, it is often helpful to reference the requirement for this type of validation on the edit and validation form without explicitly reiterating the codes or ranges.

For example, in the case of the SUPER system order identification screen layout, the participants are not required to specify that the "Order Date" must be a valid date (e.g., that a value such as 13 cannot be entered in the month area). The data element description form already contains this information in its format area. However, the participants do specify a more specialized, limited validation for this use of the "Order Date," requiring that it be compared against the "Entry Date." In addition, the participants note that in the case of the data element "Terms," the value must match one of those set forth on the data element description form.

Complete the Function Description

The function description form provides summary information about a screen or report function (see Fig. 9-8). In the JAD/Design document, it will introduce the material presented for each function. Whereas a single function could have multiple

---

FUNCTION DESCRIPTION

Function Name: Add an Order

Estimated Volume: 75–100/day (peak September–December)

Function Narrative: This function provides the capability to enter and validate new orders. The customer placing the order must already exist on file (see "Add a Customer") prior to the entry of order data. If the customer number is not known, this function may be accessed via the "Customer Number Lookup" function. The three screen layouts for this function are presented in the following order:

- Order Identification
- Order Line Items
- Order Specifications (only presented in the event that a "specialty item" is entered on the Order Line Items screen)

After validating the data, the system performs the two processing steps of pricing the order and performing an automatic credit check.

Security/Distribution:

Sales administrator	Authority granted
Sales representative	Authority granted
Sales manager	Authority granted
Credit manager	(denied)
Branch manager	Authority granted
Regional manager	(denied)
Marketing analyst	(denied)
Vice president, sales	(denied)

Figure 9-8 Sample function description.

screen or report layouts and corresponding screen edit and validation forms, a function has only one function description form. For example, the SUPER system function "Add an Order" has one function description form, although it has three layouts and corresponding edit and validation forms. The function description form has three major sections: the function narrative, the estimated volumes, and the security/distribution sections.

Function narrative.   The function narrative's main role is to explain the function purpose. The session leader typically asks the participants to dictate to the analyst one or two sentences explaining for what purpose(s) and in what contexts the organization will use the function.

The function narrative is also used to describe any peculiarities about the function flow and related manual or system processing. The session leader asks the participants to discuss how the users will arrive at the function, what the sequence of processing events will be within the function, and what will occur when the function has been completed. The participants record any deviations from a standard sequence of events, which is typically: select function from menu, process screen layout as specified on the edit and validation form, or generate report and return back to the menu.

In order to define the function flow for a given function, the session leader prods the participants with such questions, as: Are there any manual processing steps or other system functions that are integral to performing this function? If there are multiple events to this function, such as multiple layouts or a combination of layouts and processing routines, in what order do they occur? What happens when the function has been completed? Does control remain with the function, transfer to another function, or return to the menu? If the participants arrive at conclusions that deviate from the standard function flow, they provide a description for the analyst to include within the function narrative.[7]

Estimated volumes.   After completing the function narrative, the participants address the estimated volumes area on the function description form. This information will greatly assist the technical team in their system architecture and database design efforts. How many times within a meaningful time frame will the users select the function? The meaningful time frame varies with the function. For a frequently performed function, the estimate may be expressed in terms of number of times per hour or day. For less frequently used functions, it may be number of times per week or month. If significant peak periods are anticipated, the participants indicate when these periods are expected to occur in addition to their estimated volumes. The analyst records the volume estimates.

Security/distribution.   Security/distribution is the third item covered on the function description form. The JAD/Design participants identify the classification of user who is to be allowed access to a screen function. In the case of a report, the participants identify either to whom the report is distributed or, in the case of an "on-demand" report, who is allowed to request the report.

The session leader asks the participants to agree on a standard set of user classifications during their discussion of the first screen or report function within the JAD/Design. These classifications are then maintained for the remaining functions. The participants typically utilize the user types developed during the definition of scope. In the case of a multi-JAD/Design project, consistency of user classifications

---

[7]The function flow is sometimes documented in diagram format instead of text.

among JAD/Designs should be maintained. The participants review each user classification and specify whether that type of user has authority to utilize the function or whether authority is to be denied. The analyst records the security decisions.

SPECIFY PROCESSING REQUIREMENTS

When the group identifies the need to specify processing requirements—be they procedures, logic, or calculations—they do so on processing requirements sheets (see Fig. 9-9). These sheets specify whatever system processing is not already noted either on the edit and validation forms for screens or the function description form.

Apart from the heading, the processing requirements sheets are blank forms. The way in which the participants and session leader structure the sheets will vary with the nature of the requirements. In the case of procedures or logic, the participants and session leader often select bullet-format text, high-level pseudo-code, or flow diagrams to express the requirements. In the case of calculations, a combination of text and mathematical formulas may be most appropriate.

For long, complex processing requirements, the session leader may ask a participant to develop a first draft of the processing requirements sheet outside the session. Whenever possible, this would be anticipated and accomplished during JAD/Design customization. The participants then review and refine the requirements in session. For smaller, less involved processing requirements, such as calculations for a report, the session leader typically writes the requirements on a transparency or flip chart as the participants define them in session.

DEFINE INTERFACE REQUIREMENTS

During the JAD/Design session, the participants analyze and make decisions about the system interfaces (including data extracts) and document them on an interface description form (see Fig. 9-10). An interface exists any time data are shared automatically (i.e., without having to be reentered manually) between the system being designed and another, external system. The interface description form identifies the nature and direction of the interface, the frequency of the interface, the data elements involved, and any special notes or reminders about the interface. As the participants define the interface information, the session leader documents the decisions on a preformatted interface description transparency.

Identify the Interface

The participants begin the discussion by identifying the interface. The session leader asks the participants to give the interface a name that describes the type or use of data being shared between systems. The participants also specify which of the systems is the originating or sending system and which is the receiver of the data. The same two systems may have multiple interfaces, either because more than one type of data is being passed or because of the bidirectional nature of the interface.

PROCESSING REQUIREMENTS

Function Name: Generate Product Sales Summary Report

- The "Regional Category Sales Total" figure is calculated for each region as follows:

  For each product category

  —Sum up all "Line Item Total" amounts on orders with an "Entry Date" that falls within the reporting period (quarterly basis).

- The "Regional Sales Total" figure is calculated for each region as follows:

  —Sum up all order totals within an "Entry Date" that falls within the reporting period (quarterly basis).

- The "Regional Category Sales Percent" figure is calculated for each region as follows:

  "Regional Category Sales Total"

     "Regional Sales Total"

  .
  .
  .

Figure 9-9   Sample processing requirements.

Estimate Interface Frequency

The session leader then asks the participants to estimate the frequency of the interface. How current must the data be? How often should the data be updated? If there is an event or other system function that should trigger the interface (rather than basing the interface solely on time), this is noted as well.

INTERFACE DESCRIPTION

Interface Name: Extract Customer Credit Data from A/R

System From: Accounts Receivable System

System To: SUPER System

Estimated Frequency: Weekly

Data Elements: Cust No
                            Credit Limit Amt
                            Receivable Amt
                            Credit Warning Flag

Notes: (not applicable)

Figure 9-10 Sample interface description.

Specify Interfacing Data Elements

The participants also list the data elements that are to be passed between the systems. The data element names are those used within the system being designed in the JAD, rather than those of the external system. The data elements are not placed in any particular order on the interface description form. During the follow-on technical effort, the technical team will develop more detailed interface specifications that will include the data element order and any sizing adjustments or manipulation of the data required, as well as the need for specific summary data to be passed between the systems for audit and control purposes (e.g., number of records sent).

The interface description form has an area in which the participants may add clarifying notes or comments about the interface. For example, the area may be used to specify that the interface data must be summarized by a certain category or otherwise manipulated.

DOCUMENT ISSUES AND CONSIDERATIONS

Over the course of the session, numerous issues and considerations may arise. They are handled in exactly the same fashion during the JAD/Design as they are during the JAD/Plan (see Chap. 6).

CONCLUDE SESSION PHASE

The session leader concludes the session phase by reviewing with the participants what they accomplished. He or she asks the participants for feedback on the results and tries to ensure that all participants accept the decisions made. This review fortifies the feelings of teamwork, participant ownership, and commitment. The session leader may distribute a questionnaire for the participants to complete. This will help to obtain constructive feedback on the participants' reaction to the session and will enable the organization to learn from experience with the JAD methodology (see Chap. 12).

The session leader and participants may also begin to plan the JAD/Design wrap-up task of developing the executive sponsor presentation. They may assign presentation sections to various participants and develop a schedule for accomplishing the presentation preparation tasks. Finally, the session leader may provide the participants with positive feedback as to how well they performed as a group and how creative their ideas were. This "pat on the back" is usually well deserved, and helps to end the session on an upbeat note. The participants will return to their regular work locations enthusiastic about the project. They will spread the word through the organization about the value and benefits of the new system and of JAD.

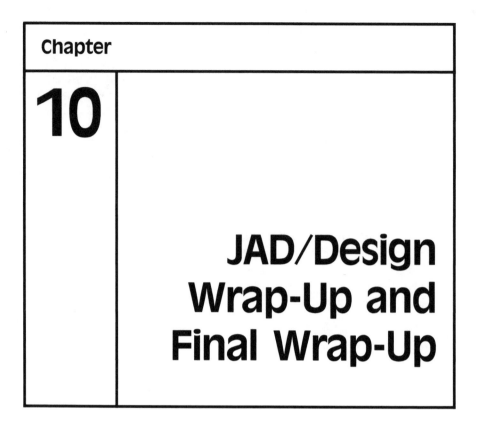

Chapter

10

JAD/Design Wrap-Up and Final Wrap-Up

JAD/DESIGN WRAP-UP

The prototype, the document, the executive sponsor presentation—the production of these three formal outputs characterizes the JAD/Design wrap-up phase. The goal of JAD/Design wrap-up is to communicate effectively and accurately the results of the session and to obtain executive sponsor approval of the design.

All of the JAD/Design session participants have some tasks to perform during the JAD/Design wrap-up phase (see Fig. 10-1). However, the main JAD players during this phase are the analysts, session leader, and information systems representatives. The user representatives' involvement is kept to a minimum in order to allow them to catch up on their other responsibilities. The number of days needed for JAD/Design wrap-up will vary, based on the system size and complexity, the amount of time allocated for participant review of the document and prototype, as well as the staffing levels for the wrap-up tasks. However, a typical JAD/Design wrap-up phase lasts between 7 and 15 workdays (refer to Chap. 6 for estimating data).

Following are the major tasks performed during JAD/Design wrap-up:

- Complete JAD/Design document.
- Develop prototype.

Participant	Typical Responsibilities
Analysts	Complete document; review document; update document; review prototype; participate in executive sponsor presentation.
Executive sponsor	Participate in executive sponsor presentation; review and approve document.
Information systems representatives	Develop prototype; review prototype; update prototype; review document; participate in executive sponsor presentation.
Session leader	Complete document; facilitate document and prototype review sessions; oversee prototype development and executive sponsor presentation development efforts; participate in executive sponsor presentation.
Specialists	Participate in executive sponsor presentation.
User representatives	Develop and participate in executive sponsor presentation; review document and prototype.

Figure 10-1   JAD/Design wrap-up participant responsibilities.

- Review JAD/Design document and prototype.
- Present results to executive sponsor.
- Obtain executive sponsor approval.

Complete JAD/Design Document

When the JAD/Design wrap-up phase begins, the results of the session phase are recorded in a combination of flip charts, transparencies, and handwritten notes. During JAD/Design wrap-up, the analysts enter all of this material into the documentation system; frequently, they are assisted part time by the session leader. The analysts and session leader may be required to expand on abbreviations or to embellish slightly bullet-item descriptions. However, it is not their task to create completely new wording or to reformat any of the session outputs. The goal is to make the formal document as familiar to the participants as possible in order to facilitate their review of the document and retain participant ownership.

In addition to entering the session results into the documentation environment, the analysts and session leader create a title page, table of contents, introduction to the JAD/Design document, and separate introductions to the major document sections. See Fig. 10-2 for a sample title page. In the case of a multi-JAD/Design project, the title page should contain both the system name and the JAD/Design name. It is advisable to place the word "DRAFT" on the title page, if not on all pages of the initial document. This will prevent confusion when changes to the document are made as a result of the review session.

Appendix D shows a sample table of contents and illustrates the order in which the JAD/Design results are typically presented in the document. Although this table of contents shows five major document sections plus appendixes, any given JAD/Design document may actually contain fewer sections and some different appendixes. For example, if the design being documented has no system interfaces, the interface section of the document is eliminated.

Processing routines may be presented as a separate section of the document or as a supplement to the function description in the external design section of the document (along with an associated screen or report function). For example, report calculations and processing requirements are more clearly presented in the external design section as part of the report function that they describe.

In some cases, the data elements section is spun off into a separate binder. This is particularly appropriate in the case of a multi JAD-Design project where the data elements section may be shared by all of the JAD/Designs as a central data repository.

The introductions to the document and its individual sections help those individuals who did not participate in the JAD/Design to understand the document. Whereas the document introduction provides an overall road map to the document, the separate section introductions provide greater detail about each section's contents and forms.

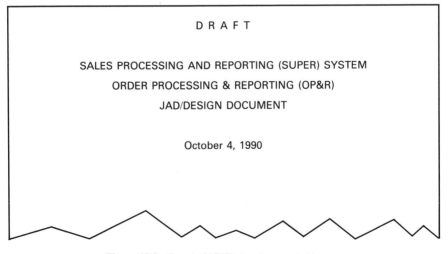

Figure 10-2 Sample JAD/Design document title page.

Develop Prototype

A prototype provides an excellent vehicle for further validating the design before making the comparatively large dollar and time investment in implementing the full-scale system. The tangible look and feel of the system come across to users of a prototype much more forcefully than pictures of the screens ever could.

The prototype also can be an education and communications tool; it is an extremely effective way to demonstrate the system to the executive sponsor and anyone else who did not participate directly in the JAD/Design sessions. For example, when new members to the technical team begin the project, they will have to learn about the system they will be building. Certainly the JAD/Design document will be their authoritative guide to the details of the system. However, the prototype can provide them with an effective orientation to the design.

The information systems representatives are usually assigned the task of developing the prototype. They often have expertise in the prototyping tool used by the organization and can develop the prototype while the analysts and session leader develop the draft document. The session leader may supervise the development of the prototype.

Before any work is done on the prototype, the extent or scope of the prototype is defined. Often, an organization will develop standards governing the scope of a prototype: Should all screens be included? How much edit and validation should be implemented? Should navigation be included (e.g., selecting from the menu)? What about error processing? In the absence of organizational standards, the executive sponsor and all JAD/Design participants should be asked for their approval of the prototype scope.

The information systems representatives develop and test the prototype. In addition, they write a brief handbook on how to use the prototype that will include how to access the prototype, what the prototype can do (the scope of the prototype) and how to exit properly from the prototype.

Review JAD/Design Document and Prototype

All of the JAD/Design participants are requested to review the completed JAD/Design document and the prototype. The purpose of the review is to ensure the quality of the document and prototype, as well as the quality of the design itself. It gives each participant an opportunity to reflect further on his or her decisions and to scrutinize the resulting output.

The document review task is typically approached in one of two ways. In either case the participants are asked to review the document on their own and submit any suggested changes to the analysts and session leader by a specified date. However, in one case a review session involving all of the participants is scheduled in advance, regardless of the changes submitted. The session may be cancelled if there are no significant changes to discuss. The other alternative is to call a review session only if material changes are submitted (i.e., they are more significant than corrections of typographical errors). Of course the first alternative is usually preferable because all participants have ample notice to set aside the scheduled time.

When the participants come from all corners of the globe, a review meeting is usually impractical. However, a prescheduled conference call can be an effective substitute. In this case, visual aids of the suggested changes may be faxed to the participants.

The analysts and session leader distribute a copy of the draft document to each of the JAD/Design participants. They attach a cover memo that asks the participants to review the document, clearly note any suggested changes on a separate piece of paper, and return the updates to the analysts or session leader at a specified location on or before a given date. If a review session is planned, the memo also states the date, time, and place of the session.

The suggested changes form the agenda for the review session. The session leader facilitates the discussion to analyze and make decisions about the participants' suggested changes. The analysts record the decisions and, subsequent to the review session, update the document accordingly. The "DRAFT" designation is then deleted from the document. One copy of the document is reserved for the executive sponsor's approval (see the discussion on obtaining executive sponsor approval below). Once approved, copies of the "FINAL FORM" document may be distributed to the technical team and redistributed to the JAD/Design participants. (Usually, the changes are so minor that the participants pencil them into their draft copies and do not receive a new copy.)

The prototype review process is similar to the document review: viewing the prototype, deciding on changes, and implementing the changes. All of the JAD/Design participants are asked to view the prototype. This may be accomplished either individually—with each participant sitting in front of a screen at his or her convenience—or as a group—with the screen image projected for all to see. When the viewing is held in a group forum, it is frequently scheduled in conjunction with the document review session.

As the participants review the prototype, they are asked to note any suggestions for changes. These changes are discussed in a prototype review session, which is typically scheduled in conjunction with the document review session. Because changes to the document will frequently affect the prototype, and vice versa, it is helpful to discuss potential changes to both of these outputs at the same meeting.

The prototype developers take notes on any changes to the prototype agreed upon by the participants. They then update the prototype, retest it, and modify the handbook, if necessary.

Present Results to Executive Sponsor

The JAD/Design participants present their design to the executive sponsor. The purpose of the presentation is to explain the design results, obtain input, and gain his or her informal approval. The presentation usually covers three major topics:

🖊 JAD perspective and results
🖊 Design results
🖊 Project status

The session leader often begins the presentation by reporting how much was accomplished during the JAD and how well the group performed during the session. The session leader may provide statistics of the number of functions that were designed and may comment on the degree of complexity and innovation entailed in the design process. The users then take over for the bulk of the presentation. One or more of the user representatives present the design to the executive sponsor. This part of the presentation may become highly interactive as the executive sponsor and users discuss how the design will service their current and future requirements.

Typically, the users present the JAD/Design requirements and workflow diagram first. These are usually shown on transparencies. The users then guide the executive through the screens and reports that they designed. They discuss the purpose of each function, how it will handle the organization's current and future needs, and any other relevant facts, such as navigation exceptions and processing summaries. During this part of the presentation, the prototype may be projected on a large screen and used as a visual aid. In the absence of a prototype, transparencies of the screen and report layouts may be used.

Once the users and executive sponsor have completed their review of the design, the information systems representative or project manager reviews the project status. He or she explains what has been achieved to date and what still lies ahead. The information systems presenter then summarizes the results of the executive sponsor presentation and concludes the meeting.

Obtain Executive Sponsor Approval

Although the executive sponsor usually provides an informal approval of the design during the executive sponsor presentation, an explicit approval in the form of a signature is a useful and important mechanism. It adds authority to the document and officially establishes the JAD/Design document as the system's requirements and external design specifications. No changes may be made to the contents of the document or the decisions described therein without the written authorization of the executive sponsor. This forms the basis of an effective change management and control policy.

The session leader or analyst writes a cover letter to the executive sponsor, presenting the final form JAD/Design document. The letter specifies that the executive sponsor's signature in the designated space at the bottom signifies that he or she accepts the contents of the JAD/Design document as part of the project baseline. At the bottom of the letter there is a signature and date line for the executive sponsor's use.

Occasionally, the executive sponsor approves the major portion of the design but requests a few changes. This may be due to external factors of which the participants were not aware, participant oversight, or executive sponsor creativity.

Such alterations usually arise during the executive sponsor presentation while the users are presenting the design. These changes may be directly entered into the document before it is distributed as the final version, or they may be written up in the organization's change request format and attached to the cover letter for the executive sponsor's signature.

Once approved, the JAD/Design document becomes a communications vehicle, reminding the participants about what they decided and informing nonparticipants about the design. The JAD/Design document will also serve as a blueprint and reference for the technical team who will build the system.

FINAL WRAP-UP

In the case of a multi-JAD/Design project, a final wrap-up is performed subsequent to the last JAD/Design wrap-up phase. The goal of final wrap-up is to further ensure design quality across JAD/Designs.[1] The session leader, analysts, information systems representatives, and a few key user representatives from the JAD/Design sessions review the JAD/Design documents and the prototype, checking for inconsistencies and awkward processing or data flows. This review primarily focuses on the points of interface among the JAD/Design scopes. The final wrap-up participants concentrate on checking the workflows, issues, considerations, and menus. The prototype is particularly helpful in validating a smooth and consistent system flow.

Once final wrap-up has been completed, the JAD stage of the project is over. The project now takes on a technical flavor as it proceeds through technical program and database design, code generation, and testing. The users are trained, and the system is finally put into operation. What began as a vague system concept and various individuals' good, but sometimes conflicting, ideas has been crystallized into a sound system design with the potential to contribute significantly to the organization's success.

---

[1]Prior to this point, JAD mechanisms have been in place to try to maintain consistency across JAD/Designs. During JAD/Plan, the participant selection task and the JAD/Design scope definition task contained JAD/Design consistency considerations. During JAD/Design, the top-down analysis and data element magnetics helped to maintain consistency as well. In addition, the JAD considerations and issues helped one JAD to communicate requirements and decisions to another JAD.

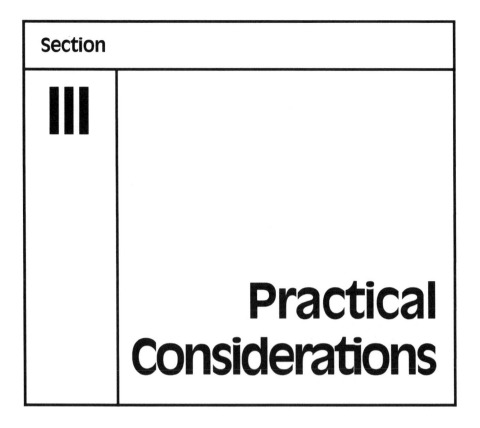

Section

III

Practical Considerations

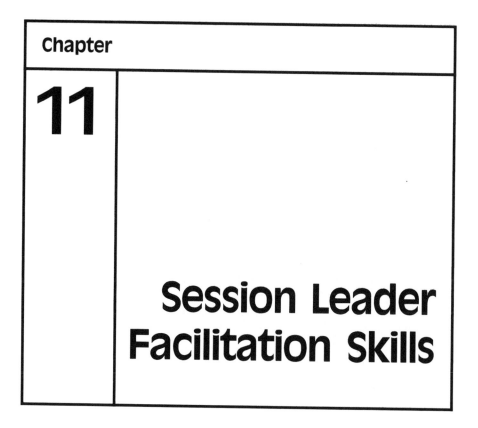

Chapter

11

Session Leader Facilitation Skills

"Just be yourself." What a great piece of advice—as long as you also know what you are doing. The individual who is natural, confident, *and* capable invariably is a success. This is particularly true of facilitating a JAD group session. The session leader who masters the JAD methodology, comfortably manages the discussion, competently handles the people issues, and is natural to boot is a real winner.

MASTER THE METHODOLOGY

Most of this book is devoted to describing the methodology—the activities, phases, tasks, participants, visual aids, output formats, and underlying concepts that make up JAD. An effective session leader not only knows what all of the JAD elements are but also understands what purpose each element serves within the overall scheme of software development.

MANAGE THE DISCUSSION

The session leader manages the JAD discussions. He or she ensures that each topic is covered thoroughly without rehashing the issues or veering off on tangents. The discussions must stimulate and hold participant interest. For any given JAD topic, the session leader guides the discussion through the following steps (see Chap. 3 for more information on the session format):

- Task presentation
- Idea generation
- Evaluation
- Commitment

Although the session leader is at all times involved in the discussions, his or her level of vocal participation ebbs and flows. As Fig. 11-1 shows, the session leader tends to dominate the task presentation step. This is when he or she identifies and explains the task under consideration. During idea generation and evaluation, the session leader encourages the participants to do most of the talking, only jumping into the discussion at critical points (see below). Questions are the predominant form of session leader participation during these two steps. The session leader takes charge again during the commitment step in order to help conclude and summarize the topic.

How to Ignite a Discussion

An important prerequisite to sparking discussion is to define clearly the task at hand. If the participants are puzzled or uncertain about the topic, they will be reluctant to generate ideas and voice opinions. The session leader must be explicit in describing the topic of discussion, explaining how it fits into the overall picture and clarifying the JAD formats. The session leader then encourages the participants to develop and express their ideas on the topic. Some techniques that help include the following:

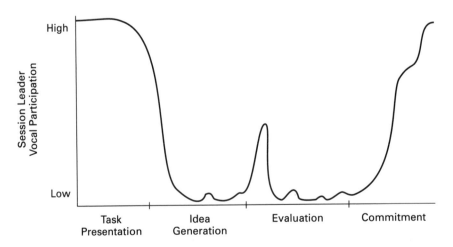

Figure 11-1 Graph of session leader vocal participation throughout discussion.

* Ask probing questions (What are some of the customer complaints about how you currently handle their orders?).
* Provide sample outputs (This is a completed workflow diagram from JAD XYZ . . .).
* Contribute lead-in answers (What data elements should we place on the "Add an Order" screen? How about starting off with order number?).

Having Ignited the Discussion, Don't Blow It Out

Once a discussion gets underway, the session leader should encourage the participants to take over. Rather than continuing to dominate the session, and in effect, stifle it, the session leader fades into the background at this point. He or she becomes the session tuner, listening intently and "tweaking" the discussion when it is required. The session leader pays close attention to ensure that there is full participation, and that the discussion stays both within the scope of the JAD and on the current topic.

Obtain Full Participation

Full participation does not mean that each participant must say something about every topic. Sometimes people have nothing to add to what has already been said. Full participation means that everyone has the opportunity to contribute; no one is being squeezed out. Each participant was selected for the JAD session in order to provide a distinct perspective or expertise. If certain participants fail to contribute to the discussions, that perspective may not be represented in the outcome.

How do you recognize a problem with full participation if you don't require everyone to talk all the time? Sometimes, body language will be the key. You may notice that a person is about to say something when another, quicker or more dominant participant jumps in ahead and starts talking. Another clue is when a participant remains silent even when the discussion centers on his or her area of expertise. In most cases where full participation is not being achieved, the cause may be traced to "people issues" such as a particularly shy or dominant participant personality (see discussion below). On occasion, the problem is rooted in insufficient participant understanding of the task being considered.

Stay Within Scope and on the Topic

Some session leaders mistake staying within the JAD scope for staying on the current topic. Such a mistake may turn the session into a free-for-all, allowing the participants to fling the discussion from one end of the JAD scope to the other. Although many of the ideas generated in a free-for-all may be very good, either the task at hand does not receive adequate consideration or the entire session schedule may be derailed. Since neither consequence is desirable, the session leader must get the group to recognize a discussion gone astray and document the topic as a JAD consideration or jot it down on the agenda to be discussed at a later, more appropriate time within the session.

How to Conclude a Discussion

Some participants could chat about a topic and its many implications ad infinitum. Although this may be fun and intellectually stimulating for some, it is not the most productive way to design a system. It is the session leader's responsibility to recognize when the topic has been adequately covered and to call for a conclusion.

There are three major types of JAD conclusions: a decision, an issue, and a consideration. At some point in the discussion, the session leader either recognizes a consensus, realizes that there is insufficient information or authority to finalize a decision, or notices that the discussion has wandered. Whatever the type of conclusion, the session leader tests to see if the participants are in agreement (e.g., Do we agree on this output? Should we obtain the executive sponsor's approval on this point? Are we out of scope here?). In testing a decision, he or she helps to ensure consistency with past decisions (e.g., Does this satisfy all of the previously defined requirements?). The session leader summarizes the results and ensures that they are documented. He or she then asks the participants to confirm or refine the conclusion.

COMPETENTLY HANDLE THE PEOPLE ISSUES

The session leader must handle the people issues that may arise. He or she is not looking for constant agreement and a lasting peace among participants; differences of opinion can be a positive force that spurs the group on to more creative alternatives. The session leader is, however, aiming to generate teamwork, cooperation, and common goals among the participants.

Diagnosing People Issues

One of the most difficult aspects of handling people issues is accurately diagnosing the problem. Since people issues are often disguised and have a multitude of causes and manifestations, what on the surface may seem to be a substantive disagreement may underneath be interpersonal. Take, for example, the case of the information systems representative who was repeatedly a negative element in the session discussions. She would roll her eyes and shake her head at other people's comments. In addition, she adamantly defended her ideas based on the system being replaced. On the surface, one would think that this individual simply liked the status quo and was resistant to change. However, the session leader hypothesized that instead this was a people issue. The information systems representative had in fact been one of the systems analysts who designed the original system. The session leader guessed that she was taking the proposed changes as personal criticism, letting them deflate her ego.

Whenever the substantive disagreements seem out of proportion to the issues, the session leader should look beneath the surface for the real problem. A session leader may notice that there are too many disagreements or negative comments on the part of one person, or that a person seems to be digging his heels in on one issue, stubbornly ignoring others' ideas, or that the person is consistently late for session, dominating the discussion, or simply not participating at all.

Solving the Problem

Once a possible people issue is identified, the session leader must try to determine the cause of the problem. Is the individual exhibiting problem behavior due to political motivation, ego sensitivity, an ulterior motive, or personality clash with another participant? The session leader hypothesizes on the source of the problem and then develops solutions to address it. When developing solutions, the session leader should be understanding and tactful. Although confronting the problem behavior head-on can be effective in some situations, it is not the only way to overcome a problem. In fact, the heart-to-heart, "we have a problem" chat can, in some situations, put the "problem" individual on the defensive and add insult to injury.

Here are some alternatives to confrontation:

- **Nonverbal approach**. To elicit a shy person's participation during a discussion, the session leader may move toward the person, make eye contact, and use questioning, open-palm gestures.
- **Humorous approach**. To encourage participants to arrive at the sessions on time, the session leader may "award" the latest participant some item (I've seen everything from a plastic dead chicken to a pineapple) that sits in front of the latecomer during the session until someone even later arrives.
- **Indirect approach**. In the case of the ego-sensitive information systems representative, the session leader decided to try to build up her ego in and out of session. The session leader asked her to provide solutions to some of the less controversial JAD tasks and called on her expertise whenever possible. By utilizing this person's ideas, the session leader was able to restore her confidence and transform her negative attitude into constructive, positive participation.

Let Good Judgment Prevail

When some new session leaders try to tackle the people issues, they get so caught up in facilitation rules, textbook symptoms, and generic solutions that they forget to use their judgment. Although books on facilitating meetings can provide valuable insight and advice, there is no substitute for good judgment.

An effective session leader handles each situation on its own merits, with understanding, tact, and maturity. Although there are definitely disruptive participants who attempt to test the session leader and take advantage of every situation, I have found these individuals to be in the minority. What I have found is that some basically cooperative participants will at times be disruptive to the JAD. For example, a participant pressured by demands outside the JAD may arrive late or forget to follow up on issues. If the session leader is heavy-handed in dealing with these individuals (treating them like naughty children), they tend to get more disruptive. If, on the other hand, the session leader appeals to their sense of cooperation, pointing out how the behavior is causing the group difficulty, the disruptive behavior usually disappears.

IT'S A MATTER OF STYLE

Let's say you are a session leader who has mastered the JAD methodology, can manage the discussions, and can handle the people issues. In order to be a shining success, you still need your own natural style. A style is something every session leader has to acquire individually. The goal is to avoid mimicking someone else. Instead, the novice session leader should seek out a style that is comfortable for his or her personality.

Some people develop a "warm, fuzzy teddy bear" style, some are great comedians, others have a more direct, down to business approach. The most effective session leaders have a basic style but can switch styles to adjust to the situation. For example, the person with a direct basic style can inject humor to lighten up a particularly long, difficult session day; likewise the warm, fuzzy leader can take a more get down to business approach if the participants become giddy, distracted, or impatient. To the seasoned session leader or the person with excellent interpersonal skills, switching to adjust to the situation is second nature. To others, it becomes second nature with experience.

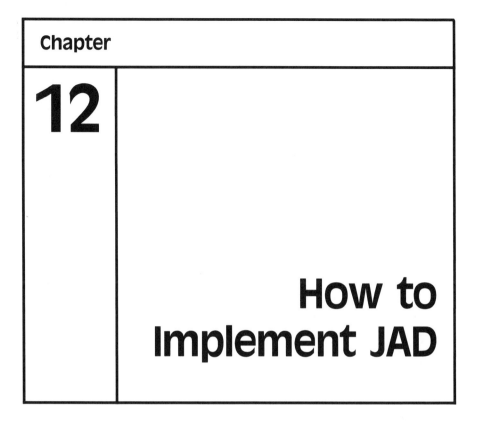

Chapter

12

How to
Implement JAD

Watching the Wimbledon tennis matches invariably inspires me to run over to my local tennis courts and play a set of tennis. I have new strategies to try, shots to perfect, and a newly affirmed vow to run down every ball, no matter how impossible a return it seems (yes, even the lobs). Without fail, I play my *worst* tennis all year right after Wimbledon. Although I have plenty of ideas for improving my tennis game, I lack the knowledge of how to implement those improvements.

Such is the case with methodologies. Unless a methodology is well implemented within an organization, the improvements that it offers may never be realized. As a consultant, I repeatedly encounter organizations that have made rational, well-researched decisions to adopt a software development methodology. They purchase and distribute thick binders that explain the new standards to the information systems professionals, only to find later on that the new methodology is either not being used correctly or not being used at all. So, how should you effectively implement JAD within your organization? I recommend a four-step approach:

- Perform a pilot project.
- Determine the nature of the JAD support group.

- Incorporate JAD into the software development life cycle.
- Extend JAD use.

PERFORM A PILOT PROJECT

The purpose of a pilot project is twofold. First, it helps an organization to test JAD for itself. You may like what you have read about JAD in this book. You may even have spoken to JAD participants who rave about the methodology. However, before you jump in with both feet, you want to make sure that JAD is everything it claims to be. After all, seeing is believing. The second purpose of a pilot project is to obtain internal organizational support for JAD. A pilot project employs the "puppy dog" sales approach—Take it home and live with it for a while; you can always return it—to generate enthusiasm and support within the information systems group and user communities. Rather than having yet another methodology rammed down their throats, they are able to experiment with JAD to see if they like it.

The three steps to perform a pilot project are the following:

- Select the appropriate pilot project.
- Test JAD.
- Evaluate JAD.

Select the Appropriate Pilot Project

In choosing the pilot project, you should take a number of factors into account. The system selected should serve multiple users in order to capitalize on JAD's group dynamics. It should incorporate many user interfaces (i.e., screens and reports), as they are more fun and rewarding to design than extensive processing routines. I usually recommend a small to medium-sized system of moderate complexity. It strikes a balance between testing JAD (putting it through the wringer) and obtaining good, fast feedback.

In selecting the pilot project for your organization, you should also consider the probable participants. It is advantageous to have a preponderance of individuals who are flexible, enthusiastic achievers. Although some of the pilot's participants may be skeptical of the new techniques, they should at least be open-minded enough to give JAD a chance.

Test JAD

Once the pilot project has been selected, the session leader must be chosen. For the test run, organizations frequently hire an experienced consultant as the session leader (and, optionally, as the analysts). This avoids the trouble and expense of training an employee before JAD has even been evaluated. The organization may choose to assign one of its own people as an apprentice to the experienced session leader. If JAD is in fact accepted as anticipated, the apprentice will be in a better position to lead JADs in the future.

When performing the pilot JAD, some organizations prefer to see the standard, ''vanilla'' JAD, with little or no tailoring to existing organizational standards. It is not until after they have completed the pilot project and have evaluated and accepted JAD that they consider how to tailor JAD to their own needs (see Chap. 5 for more information on tailoring JAD). Other organizations opt to tailor JAD to their existing standards immediately for the pilot JAD. Typically, these are organizations that have purchased CASE tools to document the requirements and external design and/or to help them with the technical, program design, coding, and testing phases of the system. They want JAD to enhance the productivity and effectiveness of these tools and thus tailor the JAD tasks and output formats to the CASE tools.

Evaluate JAD

To begin a comprehensive evaluation of JAD, start with the participants. Questionnaires and open discussions can provide JAD evaluators with a good indication of participant satisfaction with the methodology and the design it produces. A second source of data is the design itself. Evaluators can gather statistics about the accomplishments of the JAD effort. Function point analysis, pioneered by IBM, is one way of quantifying the size and complexity of the design. Simple counts of screens, reports, processing, and interfaces designed can also be used. The actual system is a third source. Evaluators can collect data about user satisfaction with the system as well as the amount of time and cost required, if any, to fix design errors.

Once the data are collected, the evaluators must analyze the results. Frequently, the first two sources of data, participant feedback and JAD statistics, are so positive that the organization decides to adopt JAD before the pilot system is operational. It is still worthwhile to collect data about the delivered system to assess the degree of success and to identify areas for improvement.

The final step in evaluating JAD is to publicize the results. In the typical organization, the qualitative results become known even before the evaluation is fully completed. The internal grapevine buzzes with informal feedback as the pilot JAD participants relate their opinions and experiences. A formal announcement of the decision should follow the evaluation through media such as the organization's newsletter, an electronic bulletin board, and speakers at organizational meetings.

DETERMINE THE NATURE OF THE JAD
SUPPORT GROUP

Determining the nature of the JAD support group is one of the early decisions that confronts an organization when it decides to adopt JAD. Who will be the organization's session leaders and analysts? Although consultants may be hired for the first few JADs, does the organization wish to rely on consultants for all of its JAD needs? Three major options have become popular.

Partially Dedicated Group

The session leader and JAD analysts may be drawn from a partially dedicated group of individuals. They may belong to the organization's application development center, user computing group, or information systems group. They may support many development products and activities. In the case of the session leader, the organization may have one fully dedicated JAD session leader or supervisor (a JAD guru of sorts), as well as a number of additional trained, experienced session leaders who may perform JADs on an occasional basis. The organization's JAD guru would be able to collect and share a wealth of JAD experience with the other, nondedicated session leaders. The analysts may be programmers and systems analysts who have been trained in JAD. They may perform the JAD for a project and stay on through the technical phases to completion.

Fully Dedicated Group

The session leader and, in some cases, the JAD analysts, may be affiliated with a full-time, dedicated JAD group. This is generally seen only in medium to large organizations with considerable software design work. The fully dedicated JAD group sometimes has an extended geographic scope, providing regional, national, or even worldwide JAD assistance.

No JAD Group

Some organizations choose not to dedicate any individuals to JAD. Generally, these organizations do not have enough design work to support JAD specialists. Instead, they choose to rely on external JAD consultants to perform their JADs. The external consultant brings a wealth of experience to the occasional JAD projects that the organization undertakes and then leaves when the projects are completed.

INCORPORATE JAD INTO THE SOFTWARE DEVELOPMENT LIFE CYCLE

Incorporating JAD into an organization's software development life cycle requires planning and forethought. It involves training, publicizing organizational standards and productivity aids, and instituting feedback mechanisms.

Provide JAD Training

An organization should consider making available various levels or paths of JAD training, depending on the JAD role an individual is to play (see Fig. 12-1). Potential session leaders require considerable education and understudy experience

Role	Recommended Training Path

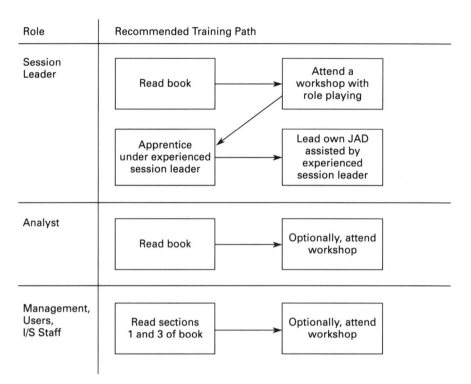

Figure 12-1   JAD education and training paths.

in order to run their own JADs effectively. They must be masters of the methodology and excellent facilitators. Analysts require a thorough understanding of the JAD methodology and its output formats. Although it is easier to run a JAD with *experienced* analysts, well-educated analysts will suffice.

A less detailed overview of JAD is appropriate for other potential JAD participants and programmers who will be implementing JAD designs. These individuals should learn about the JAD objectives, philosophy, and outputs but need not get bogged down in the details. Of course, interested individuals may wish to obtain more training than is required for their role.

Publicize Standards and Productivity Aids

The organization should make its JAD standards known and available to all individuals who will need to refer to them. In organizations where the life cycle standards are already documented, the JAD methodology should be incorporated into those standards. If organization-level tailoring of the standard JAD has occurred, particular care should be given to documenting those changes.

In addition to providing wide access to the JAD standards, the organization may wish to establish JAD productivity aids. Having standard JAD memos, forms, and presentations accessible online saves the session leader and analysts time and effort and helps to maintain organizational consistency. The session leader and analysts may use these aids in original form or modify copies to the specifics of their project.

Implement Feedback Mechanisms and Controls

Project feedback mechanisms are often incorporated in software development life cycles so that an organization can capture productivity and estimating statistics and learn from its successes and mistakes. JAD is no exception; on completion of a JAD, quantitative and qualitative results should be captured and analyzed.

For future estimating purposes, it is helpful to capture statistics regarding the estimated size of the system, the actual size of the system, significant project attributes, and the actual time and resources required to complete the JAD. The estimated size of a system is usually smaller than the actual system size, since before a project begins some scope details are invariably overlooked. When confirming a new project's estimates based on past experience, it is useful to compare the project with other projects having similar estimates (rather than comparing it with projects of similar actual size).

EXTEND JAD USE

As organizations use JAD and gain experience and confidence with it, they typically discover other types of efforts for which JAD would be useful. JAD has been applied to defining package requirements, determining package modification requirements, designed software maintenance requests, and defining office automation requirements.

Defining Package Requirements

Before an organization selects an off-the-shelf software package to serve its needs, such needs must be clearly defined. A package requirements JAD defines the requirements for a system so that the organization can determine which package will suit it the best.

A package requirements JAD differs from the standard JAD in two major ways. First, during customization, the session leader, analysts, and information systems representatives usually gain an overview of the packages available on the market. Their goal is to find out in what respects the packages differ in order to ensure that these areas are included in the session agenda. The second major difference is in the level of detail obtained during the session. Although a package requirements JAD captures the system's requirements, workflow, functions and data, it stops short of designing the screen and report layouts and the specific edits and validations. An entity-relationship diagram is often useful in determining whether a package's data structure is acceptable.

Determining Package Modification Requirements

Once an organization selects a package, it frequently has to determine whether and how to modify the package to serve its needs better. Although some of the modification requirements may be gleaned from a comparison of the original package requirements JAD document to the actual package, many of the subtleties must still be reviewed. These subtleties can often make or break the package's success in the organization.

A package modification requirements JAD runs much more smoothly and effectively when it includes someone with in-depth package expertise as a session participant. The presence of a package expert can help to avoid having to repeatedly research package facts while the session is underway. In addition, he or she may have knowledge of how other organizations solved some of the more problematic modification requests.

The session is structured in a top-down fashion, as in the case of a JAD for software design. However, instead of being designed from scratch, the package is presented and either accepted or changed. In some areas it could be cost-effective to modify the way the organization operates rather than modifying a specific aspect of the package. Changes to the organization's current policy and procedures, as well as changes to the package, should be documented.

Designing Software Maintenance Requests

In many respects, designing software maintenance requests resembles determining package modification requirements. In both cases, changes to existing software are being designed. However, software maintenance requests typically have a more limited, well-defined scope than reviewing the whole package.[1] In the case of a software maintenance request, the package or software expert is usually an internal programmer. He or she participates in the JAD as both the technical expert and the eventual implementer of the changes.

Defining Office Automation Requirements

As personal computer and workstation solutions are being sought to fill many organizations' needs, JAD is increasingly being used to define the requirements for these systems and the software tools that will run them. An office automation requirements JAD is similar in theory to a package requirements JAD. However, it is less concerned with the specific operations of the organization. The software being selected in an office automation JAD usually consists of generic tools that can be utilized for various purposes (e.g., word processing, spreadsheets). The partici-

---

[1] In some cases, the software maintenance JAD participants will have to review much of the system in order to determine how a change (such as a new law) will affect the various aspects of the system. I still consider this a more limited scope than in the case of an entire package modification review, since the analysis and discussion are limited to those areas affected by the specified change.

pants usually define the requirements and workflow in order to agree on which types of hardware and software tools will be utilized and in which capacities. The participants then evaluate the relative importance of numerous features of each tool. Many times, the resulting JAD document is sent to vendors and utilized as a Request for Proposal (RFP).

JUST ANOTHER WAR STORY

I vividly remember the last traditional, non-JAD requirements and external design project that I performed. As a systems analyst, I was part of a team of information systems consultants engaged by an organization to design a system central to its business. The requirements phase went very smoothly (which we mistook at the time for going very well). We flew all over the country performing one-on-one and small group interviews and had tours of the various offices and operations. Then we all came back, hashed out the various user viewpoints, shuttled among users for awhile to try and resolve the discrepancies we perceived, and published an impressively large requirements document. The users signed off on it within five business days, as requested.

Then came the external design phase. We, the information systems team, worked diligently to design the users' view of the system. It was a creative, exciting effort to apply our newly gained "expertise" to the design of the system's screens, reports, and processing. Again, we generated an impressive document and distributed it to the users. This time, however, the users did not exactly sign off on the document. Instead, in no uncertain terms they made it clear that what we had produced was *not* what they wanted.

To make a long and painful story short, our lead analyst spent many grueling days in closed-door meetings with the users. They ended up redesigning every screen and report—altering the data elements and arguing about the location of the data elements on the screen and report layouts. Toward the end of this redesign effort, one of the users had a milestone birthday. We ordered a sheet cake with "Happy Birthday Barbara" on it. Just as Barbara was about to blow out the candles, the lead analyst, who had managed to maintain his sense of humor throughout the course of the sometimes acrimonious redesign meetings, piped up and said, "Barbara, I hope that you have a very happy birthday. But I must say, this cake is all wrong for you. The 'Happy' should be placed to the left and much higher on the cake; the 'Birthday' is alright; the 'Barbara' should be to the right and lower; and you definitely need an exclamation point at the end!"

Unfortunately, the only unique aspect of this story is the lead analyst's sense of humor. Traditional software development projects assign the information systems professionals the futile task of learning the users' functions well enough to effectively (let alone productively) second-guess what they want in a system. It is no surprise that these projects are plagued by time-consuming, high-cost redesign efforts. Although the users on traditional projects are initially spared much of the time required to design the system, this savings becomes insignificant when compared with the time, cost, and aggravation incurred in trying to make the resulting design usable later in the development process (or, even worse, once the system is operational).

In contrast, the JAD users invest a relatively small amount of time up front to design the system right the first time. Guided by an experienced session leader, the users and information systems professionals define the system's objectives, requirements, and external design together in group sessions. One idea builds on the next as these individuals from different disciplines share their thoughts and concerns to generate innovative ideas. They design the system more expeditiously, reaping 20 to 60 percent productivity gains over traditional design methods. JAD draws the right people together and provides the structure, tools, and techniques to produce highly effective, synergistic solutions.

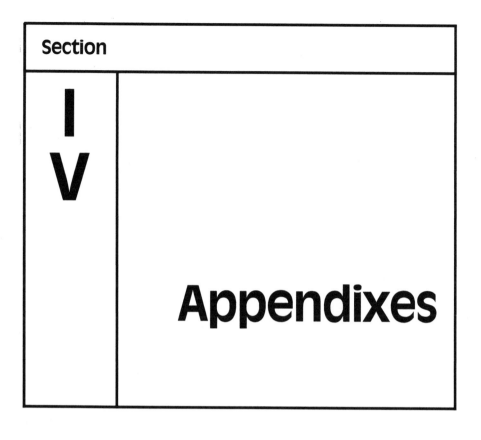

Section

IV

Appendixes

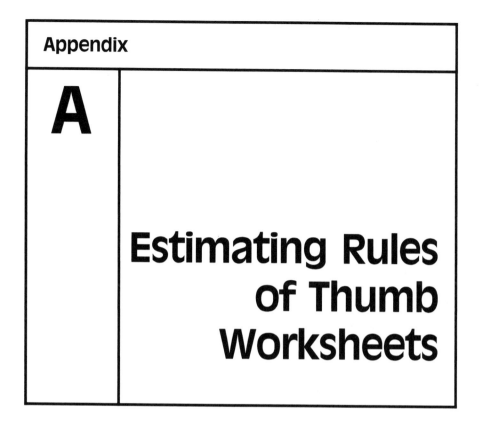

Appendix

A

Estimating Rules of Thumb Worksheets

SESSION PHASE

Step 1a. Sum number of large/complex screens plus major processing routines. _____

1b. Sum number of medium screens, medium processing routines, large reports plus interfaces. _____

1c. Sum number of small/simple screens, simple processing routines, small to medium reports.* _____

Step 2a. Divide result of step 1a by 5. _____

2b. Divide result of step 1b by 6. _____

2c. Divide result of step 1c by 7. _____

Step 3. Sum results of steps 2a, 2b, and 2c. _____

Step 4. Add to result of step 3 between 1 and 3 days for JAD/Design kickoff, requirements, scope, workflow diagram, and workflow description, as follows:

*The typical simple menu screens are collectively counted as one small simple screen for estimating purposes.

If result of step 3 is less than 3, then add 1 day.
If result of step 3 is 3–4, then add 2 days.
If result of step 3 is 5–7, then add 3 days. _____

CUSTOMIZATION PHASE

Step 1. Number of calendar workdays equal to number of session phase days (session phase, step 4). Note that this is irrespective of whether one or two analysts are assigned to the project because the session leader tends to be the critical resource. _____

WRAP-UP PHASE

Step 1. Multiply session phase days (session phase, step 4) by 3. _____
Step 2. Divide result of step 1 by number of people documenting (full time or percentage thereof). This is the amount of time to allocate for producing the document's first draft. _____
Step 3. Add 3 to 6 days for document review and update as well as executive sponsor presentation.* _____
Step 4. Add prototype development time.* _____

FINAL WRAP-UP

Step 1. In the case of a multi-JAD/Design project, add final wrap-up time to the end of the last JAD/Design. Multiply the number of JAD/Designs in the project by 2 to determine the number of calendar workdays.

_____

*Some or all of the executive sponsor presentation preparation time and the prototype development time may be scheduled in parallel with the first draft documentation tasks and would therefore not add calendar time to the wrap-up effort.

Appendix

B

Sample Completed Estimating Rules of Thumb Worksheets

SESSION PHASE

Step 1a. Sum number of large/complex screens plus major processing routines. _____2_____

1b. Sum number of medium screens, medium processing routines, large reports plus interfaces. _____11_____

1c. Sum number of small/simple screens, simple processing routines, small to medium reports.* _____9_____

Step 2a. Divide result of step 1a by 5. _____0.40_____

2b. Divide result of step 1b by 6. _____1.83_____

2c. Divide result of step 1c by 7. _____1.29_____

Step 3. Sum results of steps 2a, 2b, and 2c. _____3.5_____

Step 4. Add to result of step 3 between 1 and 3 days for JAD/Design kickoff, requirements, scope, workflow diagram, and workflow description, as follows:

*The typical simple menu screens are collectively counted as one small simple screen for estimating purposes.

If result of step 3 is less than 3, then add 1 day.
If result of step 3 is 3–4, then add 2 days.
If result of step 3 is 5–7, then add 3 days.   *5.5*

CUSTOMIZATION PHASE

Step 1. Number of calendar workdays equal to number of session phase days
(session phase, step 4). Note that this is irrespective of whether one or two
analysts are assigned to the project because the session leader tends to be
the critical resource.   *5.5*

WRAP-UP PHASE

Step 1. Multiply session phase days (Session phase, step 4) by 3. *16.5*
Step 2. Divide result of step 1 by number of people documenting (full time or
percentage thereof). This is the amount of time to allocate for producing
the document's first draft.   *6.6*
Step 3. Add 3 to 6 days for document review and update as well as executive
sponsor presentation.* (partially parallel)   *9.6*
Step 4. Add prototype development time.* (parallel)   *9.6*

FINAL WRAP-UP

Step 1. In the case of a multi-JAD/Design project, add final wrap-up time to the
end of the last JAD/Design. Multiply the number of JAD/Designs in the
project by 2 to determine the number of calendar workdays.
                                                              N/A

---

*Some or all of the executive sponsor presentation preparation time and the prototype development time may be scheduled in parallel with the first draft documentation tasks and would therefore not add calendar time to the wrap-up effort.

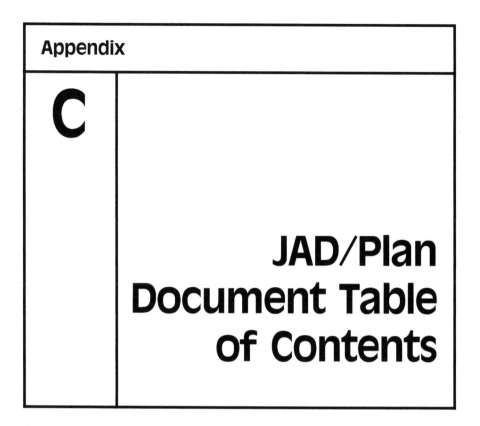

Appendix

C

JAD/Plan Document Table of Contents

1.0 INTRODUCTION

2.0 REQUIREMENTS SECTION

2.1 High-Level Requirements
Objectives
Anticipated benefits
Strategic and future considerations
Assumptions and constraints
Security, audit, and control requirements

2.2 System Scope
Business flow diagram
System users and locations
Out-of-scope functional areas

3.0 JAD/DESIGN PLANS SECTION

3.1 Participant Matrix

3.2 JAD/Design Identifications

3.3 Estimating Assumptions

APPENDIXES

A.   JAD/Plan Issues
B.   JAD/Plan Considerations
C.   List of JAD/Plan Participants

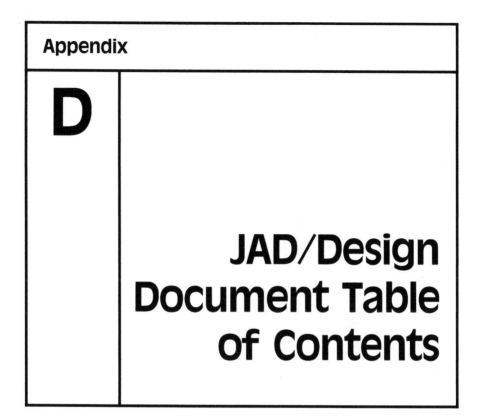

Appendix

D

JAD/Design Document Table of Contents

1.0 INTRODUCTION

2.0 REQUIREMENTS SECTION

2.1 Requirements Topics
Objectives
Anticipated benefits
Strategic and future considerations
Assumptions and constraints
Security, audit, and control requirements

2.2 System Scope
System users and locations
Workflow diagram
Workflow description
Out-of-scope functional areas

3.0 EXTERNAL DESIGN SECTION

3.1 Function 1
Function description
Screen/report layout(s)
Edit and validation(s)

3.2 Function 2
Etc.

4.0 INTERFACE SECTION
Interface descriptions

5.0 PROCESSING SECTION
Processing requirements

6.0 DATA ELEMENT SECTION
Data element descriptions

APPENDIXES

A. JAD/Design Issues

B. JAD/Design Considerations

C. List of JAD/Design Participants

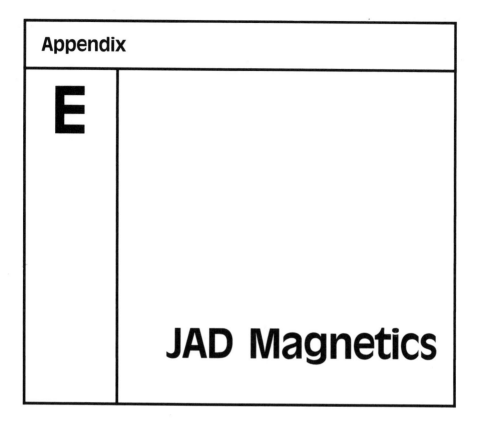

Appendix

E

JAD Magnetics

The standard JAD magnetics are vinyl rectangles with magnetic strips on the back. You can write on them with water-soluble pens (such as transparency markers) and then wash them clean to revise or reuse them. The data element magnetics measure 1.5 inches by 7.5 inches. The process blocks measure 5.0 inches by 7.5 inches. Additionally, magnetics in such shapes as computer monitors and data stores may be used along with the process blocks for the JAD diagrams, but these are not essential. One supplier of the magnetics is Ryan Screen Printing, Inc., 5412 West Burnham Street, Milwaukee, WI 53219.

Bibliography

1. Gibson, Cyrus F., and Barbara Bund Jackson, *The Information Imperative: Managing the Impact of Information Technology on Business and People*. Lexington, Mass.: Lexington Books D. C. Heath, 1987.
2. Harris, C. L., "Information Power: How Companies Are Using New Technologies to Gain a Competitive Edge," *Business Week*, October 14, 1985, pp. 108–14.
3. Huff, S. L., "Supporting Competitive Strategy with Information Technology: Customer Oriented Strategic Systems," *Business Quarterly*, 53 (Autumn 1988), 37–39.
4. Lucas, Henry C., Jr., *The Analysis, Design and Implementation of Information Systems* (3rd ed.), New York: McGraw-Hill, 1985.
5. _____, "User-Oriented Systems Analysis and Design," in *A Practical Guide to Systems Development Management*, ed. James Hannan. Pennsauken, N.J.: Auerback, 1982.
6. Martin, Charles F., *User-Centered Requirements Analysis*. Englewood Cliffs, N.J.: Prentice Hall, 1988.
7. Martin, James, *Information Systems Manifesto*. Englewood Cliffs, N.J.: Prentice Hall, 1984.
8. _____, *System Design from Provably Correct Constructs*. Englewood Cliffs, N.J.: Prentice Hall, 1985.
9. Rush, Gary, "A Fast Way to Define System Requirements," *Computerworld*, October 7, 1985, pp. 11–16.

Index